The Financial Markets of the Arabian Gulf

The Financial Markets of the Arabian Gulf

Jean-François Seznec

CROOM HELM
London • New York • Sydney

© 1987 Jean-François Seznec
Croom Helm Ltd, Provident House, Burrell Row,
Beckenham, Kent BR3 1AT

Croom Helm Australia Pty Ltd, Suite 4, 6th Floor,
64-76 Kippax Street, Surry Hills, NSW 2010, Australia

British Library Cataloguing in Publication Data

Seznec, Jean-François
    The financial markets of the Arabian gulf.
    1. Finance — Persian Gulf region
    I. Title
    332   HG187.P4
    ISBN 0-7099-5404-2

Published in the USA by
Croom Helm
in association with Methuen, Inc.
29 West 35th Street
New York, NY 10001

Library of Congress Cataloging in Publication Data
applied for:

Printed and bound in Great Britain by
Biddles Ltd, Guildford and King's Lynn

Contents

Abbreviations

AAM	Arbab Al-Maal
ABC	Arab Banking Corporation
ALBA	Aluminium Bahrain Company
APG	Advanced Payment Guarantee
APICORP	Arab Petroleum Investment Corporation
ARIG	Arab Insurance Group
ASRY	Arab Shipbuilding and Repair Yard
BAII	Banque Arabe et Internationale d'Investissements
BBME	British Bank of the Middle East
BKIC	Bahrain-Kuwait Insurance Company
CBK	Commercial Bank of Kuwait
EC	Exempt Company
FDIC	Federal Deposit Insurance Company
FSLB	Federal Savings and Loan Board
FSLIC	Federal Savings and Loan Insurance Company
GCC	Gulf Cooperation Council
GIB	Gulf Internationial Bank
IBL	Investment Banking License
KFH	Kuwait Finance House
KFTCIC	Kuwait Foreign Trading, Contracting and Investment Company
KIA	Kuwait Investment Authority
KIC	Kuwait Investment Company
KIIC	Kuwait International Investment Company
KIO	Kuwait Investment Organization
KUCLEAR	Kuwait Clearing House Company
MABCO	Manufacturing and Building Company
MEED	*Middle East Economic Digest*
MEES	*Middle East Economic Survey*
NBB	National Bank of Bahrain
NCI	National Chemical Industries
OAPEC	Organization of Arab Petroleum Exporting Companies
OBU	Off-shore Banking Unit
OPEC	Organization of Petroleum Exporting Companies
PB	Performance Bond
PIF	Public Investment Fund
RFFG	Reserve For Future Generations

RUF	Revolving Underwriting Facility
SABIC	Saudi Arabian Basic Industries Company
SAFCO	Saudi Arabian Fertilizer Company
SAMA	Saudi Arabian Monetary Agency
SAPTCO	Saudi Arabian Passenger Transport Company
SCECO	Saudi Consolidated Electricity Company
SIB	Saudi International Bank
SIBC	Saudi Investment Banking Corporation
SIDF	Saudi Industrial Development Fund
TAIB	Trans-Arabian Investment Bank
TAIC	The Arab Investment Company
UABC	United Arab Broking Company
UDT	Dar Tadine Al-Umma

Hijri/Gregorian Calendar

Hijri years	Gregorian years	
	Beginning	Ending
1397	23 December 1976	11 December 1977
1398	12 December 1977	1 December 1978
1399	2 December 1978	20 November 1979
1400	21 November 1979	8 November 1980
1401	9 November 1980	29 October 1981
1402	30 October 1981	18 October 1982
1403	19 October 1982	7 October 1983
1404	8 October 1983	26 September 1984
1405	27 September 1984	15 September 1985

Introduction

Finance is of key importance to the development of each country and the flows of funds are vital to the daily and future welfare of all the citizens. Hence, each of the governments of Saudi Arabia, Bahrain and Kuwait has put great emphasis on developing financial structures. It is a central theme of this book that the markets have evolved differently in each of these three countries because of basic political choices by their respective governments. The governments are very similar, all beduin conservatives, with one-family rule. However, each is faced with different cultural and sociological variables which have influenced each government's image of what the future must bring. It is therefore hoped that this study of financial markets will give a glimpse of the fiber of these three Arab nations.

Saudi Arabia is usually viewed as a purely capitalistic country, with freedom of investment, free capital movements in and out of the country, no taxation, subsidies to companies, and generally as a country that is pro-business. In reality, however, the Al Sauds need to unify further a very diverse population. The royal family wants to have a say in, and influence on, all aspects of society to consolidate its power. Hence, the management of the economy has slowly but thoroughly been centralized in the hands of the minister of finance, and, through him, in the hands of the King. Investments are only encouraged, and entitled to the great benefits bestowed by the government, if they fit into the scheme of development mapped out by the King and his very able technocrats. The costs of doing business are such in Saudi that it is virtually impossible to succeed in any venture against the wishes of the bureaucracy. One of the entities in charge of enforcing the master plan is the Saudi Arabian Monetary Agency. SAMA today basically embodies the views of the Minister of Finance, Mr Aba Al Khail.

A stock market has not been allowed to develop in Saudi. The only capital gathering for use in industry is through public offerings arranged by government entities who keep control of the boards and of the management. A good example is SABIC which invests heavily in the Jubail projects.

The banks are subject to more and more SAMA scrutiny. SAMA has managed an orderly Saudi-ization of the foreign-owned banks. Although the foreign parent banks still control most of the management and decisions it is very likely that control of these banks will be in Saudi hands within two or three years.

The money changers, the original bankers of the region, have been leashed and are no longer allowed to issue checkbooks, make loans, or manage deposits. They are being forced to become commercial banks, Islamic banks or just foreign exchange traders. At any rate their role has been reduced and is being subordinated to SAMA.

Islamic banking has been viewed as the great hope of the Arab world — to provide in a manner acceptable to God the financial flows needed for economic development. Surprisingly, however, Saudi has not been the cradle of this new concept. In fact, there appears to have been great suspicion on the part of the monetary agency with regard to the Islamic banks formed in Saudi. The suspicion is partly due to SAMA's fear of entities which use the name of God, claim to be the true followers of Islam and thus become hard to control. It is also due to SAMA's views on the personalities and motives of the proponents of Islamic banking in the kingdom.

Of course, the development of financial markets and of industry in general is a very hot issue. The government has to contend with the very strong religious feelings which stop any evolution of the legal system, stop the entrance of women into the labor force, and create general suspicion towards anything that can be viewed as 'riba' (often translated as 'interest'). Hence the debates are somewhat skewed in favor of the government. On the one hand the traditionalists and the 'muttawas' demand that the government be the protector of Islam and the proper way of life. On the other hand the traders, industrialists, bankers, and all entrepreneurs have to view the government as the protector of economic freedom against the reactionary forces which want to stop progress and development. The consequence is that the entrepreneurial forces cannot but follow the government directives.

In Kuwait, on the other hand, we have witnessed much more laissez-faire. Kuwait has traditionally been a nation of traders and seafarers as well as of beduins. The government appears to have a more open approach to the management of its economy. The policy was to provide the population with the benefits of high oil revenues in the form of investments abroad for use by later generations, and for the present by actual inputs of cash into the financial system. One of the favourite means of getting money to the people was to buy lands from the public at an inflated price and to resell the same land at a loss, over and over again.

This attitude greatly encouraged speculation in land, in land development companies and eventually in all companies. Banks which had financed normal activities, such as letters of credit and short-term industrial loans, became very involved in financing real estate and share speculation. The money changers, who had large amounts of cash on deposit, also became very much involved in speculation for their own account, often using the deposits of their clients and correspondent banks. Even the Islamic banks became heavily involved in speculative deals and incurred large losses in the process.

The Kuwaitis were the first Gulf citizens to develop real capital markets, with a stock exchange, investment companies, brokers, etc. The government not only closed its eyes to the creation of a parallel stock market, but some of its ministers and members of the ruling family became major players in the speculation. Companies were created for the sole purpose of speculating in shares. Eventually, in August 1982, the speculative bubble burst, bringing the markets to a virtual halt, and forcing large intervention by the government in the banks, the investment companies, the money changers, etc. As of June 1986 the crisis was not yet fully resolved but was leading to a bail out of the market by the government. To prop up at least some of the share prices, the government had to buy billions of dollars worth of shares in Kuwaiti companies and has had to deposit large amounts of funds in the commercial banks. Hence the government has now become the major owner of most sizeable economic activity in Kuwait. In other words, there has been a de facto nationalization of much of the private commercial assets. One cannot expect this situation to remain for ever, but it is most likely that in the future the Kuwaiti financial markets will be under the very close scrutiny of the ministry of finance and of the parliament.

Bahrain has had policies somewhere between that of Saudi and Kuwait. Probably because of its amazing ethnic and cultural diversity and its position at a crossroads of the Gulf, it has developed as a financial service center for the whole Gulf.

Bahrain became the base for up to 170 banks active in the Gulf, and has promoted the development of at least two major international institutions, GIB and ABC, and the creation of a large insurance company. In addition, Bahrain has allowed the creation of locally based publicly held corporations with private and widely held ownership from all over the Arabian Gulf. In its dealings with both Kuwait and Saudi, Bahrain has had to be very nimble in order to avoid antagonising the policies of each country. At the height of the Souk Al Manakh, many highly placed Kuwaitis tried to use Bahrain for speculation purposes. The monetary agency and the government managed to limit such activities without actually saying no. On the Saudi side, the Bahrain-based off-shore Banking Units (OBUs) became very active in the Kingdom. The OBUs began providing speedy and

sophisticated services to the Saudi traders and industrialists which
Saudi banks, even the foreign-owned ones, were not able to provide.
The Bahrain OBUs' activities became of great concern to SAMA who
felt it could lose some of its control over the Saudi economy. The
Bahraini authorities were able to discourage the Saudis from clamp-
ing down too hard on the activities of the OBUs by arguing that
Bahrain has only minimal resources and must have a service economy
to survive and remain stable. Underlying the whole argument is the
theory that the Saudis prefer not to have a militant Shi'a population
30 kilometers from their main oil facilities.

The future of the financial markets in Bahrain is very dependent
upon the potential success of the Gulf Cooperation Council. The GCC
could hinder the centralizing policies of Saudi Arabia. Riyadh is
heavily committed to the GCC and hence must contend with the aims
and means of the other nations in the council. If the council continues
to develop as it has in the past three years, there are good opportunities for a strong market to prosper in Bahrain.

However, one could expect that the control by SAMA of the Saudi
financial markets will not decrease. There may be a change in leadership. If King Fahad is replaced, one could expect an immediate change
in finance minister and, ergo, a change in the governorship of SAMA.
Nevertheless, the institution will not change radically. The individuals
enforcing the SAMA controls in the financial institutions may change
but the system will remain.

In Kuwait, the laissez-faire which has now been replaced by
government ownership of the institutions will slowly be restored. One
can guess, however, that the government will keep a very close control on the markets, and that it will be in a similar form to the Saudi
system.

A number of other variables will further influence the development of the markets. The Gulf is undergoing a very difficult period.
The decline in oil revenues has hit the treasuries and the amount of
money passed on by the governments to the public has decreased
substantially. There is a great deal of tension in the region because
of the endless Iran-Iraq war. The war has cost large amounts of money
to Saudi Arabia, and put great pressures on the stability of the Bahraini
and Kuwaiti governments.

The markets will now become more oriented to provide specific
services. There will be more investment banking services, such as
mergers and acquisitions, or liquidation advisory services. Again we
will witness different reactions in the three countries along the lines
of their different cultural and sociological structures.

In the following chapter we describe each market segment separately: the central banks, the commercial banks, the stock markets (with emphasis on the rise and fall of the Souk Al Manakh), the Islamic banks, the money changers, the investment companies and the insurance companies. Finally we evaluate what the future holds for the markets.

The Gulf Financial Markets
Prior to 1973

Late 1973 was a time that changed the Gulf nations for ever. The benchmark for Saudi light crude went from US$ 3.011 per barrel on 1 October 1973 to US$ 5.119 per barrel on 16 October 1973.[1] The price continued to increase until 1980 when it hit US$ 42 per barrel at the start of the Iraq-Iran war.[2] There was a sudden realization of the worth of the region and of the ability to put money where the dreams were. Visions of an Islamic renaissance became powerful incentives to develop the industrial, agricultural and also social potential of each Gulf nation.

Saudi Arabia, with the most reserves and the highest production and hence income, was also the most ambitious. The Saudis could almost see themselves as the recipient of the blessings of God and as the carrier of a revival message giving them the leadership of a conservative and nevertheless modern Islam. Prior to 1973, the region, including Saudi Arabia, was somewhat behind the times. There was little industry except that of petroleum extraction and a few small refineries for local use. Agriculture was very backward. Production was by use of uneducated cheap local labor and was limited to wheat, barley, alfalfa, dates, and a few fruits. Meat production was the domain of the beduins who provided goats, lambs, and camels. Here and there were small antiquated dairies supplementing the camel milk sold by the beduins.

In terms of finance, the markets were just as backward as the non-petroleum side of the economy. There were basically two types of financial institutions: the banks and the money changers. The money changers were, and to a lesser degree still are, a very important financial intermediary. They have always served a role somewhat akin to that of the banking families of Italy during the European renaissance.

In Saudi they provided foreign exchange services to travellers bringing all manner of currency, convertible and non-convertible.

They provided a vital service in the Haj. Pilgrims who brought their home currency or coins had to pay their daily expenses in riyals. Even in the early 1960s they were always numerous, hovering around the 200,000 mark. Their number started increasing after 1970 reaching as high as 1,003,911 in 1403(1982–3).[3] The 'hajis' (pilgrims) usually stayed from one to two months, and consequently they brought large amounts of cash which translated into a high volume of currency exchange. Profits also were high. Since the money changers were dealing in coins as well as paper, they were very skilled in handling precious metals. To this day the money changers have remained the major dealers of gold and silver bullion in the kingdom. The main money changers in Jeddah have usually been of Hadrami origin. The families involved in this trade were the Bamaoudeh, Kaki, Bin Mahfoudh, al Amoudi, Bajrai, Balahwal, and others. Another very large money changing family, the Rajhi family, originated in Najd. A branch of the family is very active in Jeddah, but the main part of their business was developed in Riyadh, by Saleh Rajhi.

In Riyadh, Rajhi was not involved in money changing before 1970. He had begun to provide semi-investment banking services. A businessman with an idea and no funds would often go to Rajhi and obtain the capital to start his company. The Rajhi family was also very much involved in land development, and Sheikh Saleh grew to be one of the richest persons in Saudi Arabia by developing large tracts of land located in what was to become the center of Riyadh.

In the Gulf the money changers were also very active. Of course they were the correspondents of the Jeddah changers, but traditionally they were involved in the Far Eastern trade, and the related precious metal trade. Their strength was very limited when compared to that of the Haj-based changers. They remained mostly involved in the local currency markets, and precious metals.

In the Gulf the money changers were competing with the banks active in the British Empire. Bahrain and Kuwait were under British rule until 1973 and 1961 respectively. The Eastern Bank, which was to become the Standard Chartered Bank, opened a branch in Bahrain in 1921, basically to service the British in Bahrain, as well as to serve the burgeoning trade business. The British Bank of the Middle East (BBME) opened a branch in Kuwait in 1941. It then also opened a branch in Bahrain in 1944 to cater for the increased business resulting from petroleum production, and the increase in import business.[4] The banks in the Gulf were the only institutions able to facilitate trade between manufacturing countries and the countries of the Gulf. The first Bahraini-owned bank, National Bank of Bahrain (NBB), was opened in 1957 by the major merchant families of Bahrain. NBB at first was managed by expatriate personnel but increased its Bahraini staff over the years until a local general manager, Mr Nooreddin Nooreddin, was named in 1980. By 1986 most of the officers and clerks were Bahraini nationals.

In Saudi, on the other hand, the banks which first started their activities were branches of banks active in other colonial empires. The first bank to open was Algemene Bank of the Netherlands, which established a branch in Jeddah in 1925. Banque de l'Indochine followed suit, but only 25 years later. The same year, 1950, the British Bank of the Middle East was able to be the first and only British bank to start operations in the kingdom. The banks active in Jeddah also opened branches on the east coast of Saudi in the 1950s. There were no foreign banks in Riyadh until King Faysal allowed First National City Bank to open a branch in the Batha part of town in November 1966, after it had opened a branch in Jeddah on 31 December 1955. The first locally owned banks also opened in Jeddah: the National Commercial Bank, owned by two former money changers, Messrs Bin Mahfoudh and Kaki, was founded in 1937; the Riyadh Bank was established in Jeddah in 1957 by a group of merchants led by the Sharbatly family.

The banks' main activity was trade finance. This business consists mostly of evaluating the credit of a merchant, opening on his behalf letters of credit to be drawn upon in an exporting country at the counter of the same bank or of a correspondent bank. The bank can then extend short-term loans to the merchant until the merchandise imported is sold. The relationships between merchants and banks were developed over the years. The banks usually wanted to be secured by mortgages on properties owned by the merchant, although all knew that such security could not be safely relied upon, as there never had been any precedent for foreclosure.

Profits made by the banks were substantial. The banks operated with low-paid clerks, often from the Indian subcontinent, and a handful of expatriate officers. The banks earned fees on the opening of the letters of credits of up to 1 per cent per quarter, took a foreign exchange commission on the settlement of the letter of credit from one currency to the local currency, and had a substantial spread on their loans. In 1974 the average cost of funds of a major foreign bank in Jeddah was 2.5 per cent and most loans were made at an interest rate of 6 to 7 per cent.

Of course the banks were also quite active in foreign exchange dealings. Foreign exchange services were necessary to provide the merchants with means to pay their obligations in local currencies while the imports were bought in British pounds, US dollars or some other major world currency. Again, since there was little competition except that of the money changers, business was good.

Communications were extremely difficult with the outside world, especially in Saudi Arabia. Hence the local management of the banks had great power to decide by itself what, how, how much and to whom it could provide credit. In 1973, there were only 31,600 telephone lines in the kingdom, equivalent to 1.02 lines for each 1,000 inhabitants.[5] Telephone service from Jeddah to the rest of the kingdom was virtually impossible, let alone to the rest of the world. Telex lines were very rare and air links were poor and unreliable.

In Kuwait and Bahrain communications were much easier. The authorities had developed networks which were the envy of all Saudis. In 1973 Kuwait had 8.35 telephone lines per inhabitant and Bahrain 5.92.[6] The telephone lines could access international lines by satellite stations. The first station was built in Bahrain in 1969, to be followed by two more, one in 1980 and one in 1983.[7] Very soon after the Second World War the British had also developed good air links between India, Bahrain, Kuwait and London. These international links were readily assimilated by these countries who already had been trading with the outside world for centuries.

The improved communications links, combined with the local tradition of merchant trading, gave Bahrain and Kuwait the lead in financial sophistication. In Kuwait, five locally owned banks had been established by 1968, which were founded by local merchants to compete with the foreign banks. Eventually even the British Bank of the Middle East was brought under Kuwaiti control in 1973. The government established some specialized institutions such as the Savings and Credit Bank as early as 1968, the Industrial Bank and the Real Estate Bank in 1973. The purpose of these specialized banks was to provide easier access to credit, especially long-term money, for the population as a whole.

Bahrain before 1973 was a fairly quiet place. The large oil revenues had not started to have an impact on the local economy. On the other hand Bahrain had been the first Gulf country to see its oil being pumped and, unlike in Saudi, the first benefits of petroleum income had been around the population for some time. By 1973 the oil production in Bahrain itself and Bahrain's share of the Abu Safah offshore field was beginning to decline, falling below 50,000 barrels per day, and the reserves were small. The government decided to diversify the economy into services and industry and laid the foundations for the start up of major industrial projects like ASRY (Arab Shipbuilding and Repair Yard Company) and ALBA (Aluminium Bahrain Co.). At the end of 1973, the financial sector had not yet developed into the large money center it was to become by 1980, but the creation of the Bahraini dinar in 1965 and the foundation in 1973 of a central monetary authority, the Bahrain Monetary Agency, were the first steps.

The foreign banks were beginning to have a presence. Citibank, Chase Manhattan Bank, and Paribas had full commercial branches. There were also some branches of banks obviously set up to cater to a definite segment of the market. For instance, Bank Melli was started to service the fairly substantial business between Iran and Bahrain which flourished before the Iranian revolution as a consequence of the important Iranian community in Bahrain. United Bank of Pakistan, Habib Bank, and Banque du Caire were able to service their respective Pakistani and Egyptian expatriates, and handle their remittances and other banking needs.

The money changers were still a main supplier for the banking needs of Bahrain. They catered for the merchants who required foreign exchange, and for the British, Indian, and other expatriates for remittances home (which includes a foreign exchange transaction dinar/pound or roupie or dollar etc.).

The oil revenues of Saudi Arabia in 1392/3 (1972/3) were Saudi riyals 2,529 million. Two years later revenues had shot up to SR 37,654 million.[8] Lacking the physical and financial infrastructure of Bahrain and Kuwait, the Saudis were unprepared for their twelve-fold increase in income. Fortunately King Faysal bin Abdelaziz Al Saud, who reigned from 1964, had more of a vision for his country than his predecessor King Saud. King Faysal surrounded himself with some well-educated and competent civil servants. He promoted his private lawyer, Sheikh Ahmed Zaki Yamani to the ministry of petroleum, placed Abdel Hadi Taher, a US-educated engineer at the head of Petromin, and named Sheikh Mohammed Aba Al Khail Minister of Finance. He also started a ministry of industry and electricity and a ministry of planning where he placed Sheikh Hisham Nazer.

Most of the ministers in charge of the various finance and economic portfolios installed by King Faysal were still in place in 1986. This stability in fact reflected the strength of the main adviser to King Faysal, the then Prince Fahad bin Abdelaziz Al Saud. After the assassination of King Faysal in 1975 Prince Fahad remained as adviser and Deputy Prime Minister under the newly appointed king, Khaled bin Abdelaziz Al Saud, and Prince Fahad was able to maintain the policies established under Faysal.

In 1974 Sheikh Aba Alkhail requested the Chase Manhattan Bank of New York to help start and manage two institutions in Saudi on behalf of the government. The first one to be founded was the Saudi Industrial Development Fund with a capital of SR 500 million, which was increased within a year to SR 3 billion. The duty of SIDF was to provide 50 per cent financing to all industrial ventures in Saudi. Sheikh Mohammed also arranged for Chase to start a privately owned joint venture bank with Commerzbank, the Industrial Bank of Japan, and 60 per cent with the Saudi public. This entity was to be named Saudi Investment Banking Corporation. It was to be the first Saudi-foreign bank in the kingdom. Unfortunately there were substantial complications at the start because of disagreement between Chase and the Saudi government on what products could be offered by the bank to the market. Originally the bank was to specialize in medium-term loans to industries to make up privately what SIDF could not lend. Eventually the bank was licensed to start operations in 1976, and was then allowed to provide medium-term loans, bonds and guarantees, open letters of credit and take wholesale deposits. In other words, SIBC could act as a wholesale bank.

At the same time King Faysal ordered the foundation of the Real Estate Fund, which became fully operational only after 1976. A government-owned agricultural bank was founded before 1972 and provided subsidies to farmers for the purchase of seeds, implements and fertilizers. The Agricultural Bank became very important after 1980, when the government launched a program of agricultural self-sufficiency.

The procedures for industrial development were put in place as early as 1973. To found any kind of commercial activity in Saudi one had to obtain a commercial registration from the ministry of commerce and industry. However, to start an industrial venture one also had to obtain an industrial license, which was issued by the ministry after a review by the Industrial Studies and Investment Center. Foreign capital was not forbidden but any foreign investment had to be approved by the Foreign Capital Investment Committee.

A comprehensive five-year development plan was drafted by Hisham Nazer in 1972, with help from Stanford Research Institute, which outlined the areas critical for the proper modernization of the kingdom. The Saudi plan was not all-encompassing and did not impose production goals on various industries. It did however define the needs for roads, harbors, telephones, telexes, airports, housing, sewage, etc. In the light of this plan the ministry of industry was thus able to accept or refuse any request for industrial projects.

In late 1975, Bechtel, the well-known engineering consulting firm, was commissioned to develop a plan for the creation of two industrial cities. The purpose was to centralize the development of petrochemical industries, and of heavy energy users, in two strategically based locations. The idea was to start from raw land so as to build the most modern and streamlined operations possible. A site near the small town of Jubail was chosen because it had large virgin buildable lands close to the oil fields and was near good deep water on the Arabian Gulf. Yanbu was chosen also for being a good harbor site on the Red Sea which could provide a suitable terminal for a trans-Arabian pipeline. The first plans for Jubail and Yanbu called for the building of a number of petrochemical plants, ethanol, methanol, ethylene, etc, as well as for the creation of high energy users, such as a direct reduction steel mill which is presently fully operational.

By 1976 it was increasingly clear that the government wanted Saudi to become a major force in all petroleum and high energy based productions. The Saudi reserves were estimated to be between 80 years and 160 years depending on the level of production. The Saudi Arabian government felt it had to take advantage of its new wealth to diversify away from being just a raw material producer. Industries that can be developed with capital and energy normally demand only limited amounts of labor and are, therefore, quite suitable for the kingdom. They do however demand a large number of highly skilled personnel and engineers who at the time were sorely lacking. It was therefore a corollary that education had to be developed. Schools and universities had to be built. Teachers had to be trained and imported. Housing had to be built for the builders of the new cities, schools, factories, housing compounds, etc.

The economic development started taking place at the same time as the building and improvement of the infrastructure of the country, which was needed to create that very development. None of the facilities could handle the enormous growth which was taking place: communications were very backward, and harbors small and inefficient. It was a very trying time for all who lived in Saudi Arabia.

The logistical and infrastructural problems mentioned earlier showed with a vengeance to all Saudis that there were great needs. There were shortages of all types of building materials, and whatever was available was of extremely poor quality. Demand for sand, cement, pipes, steel, cement blocks, tools, furniture, brought these commodities to astronomical prices. At first most of the shortages were met by imports. This, however, added considerable pressure on the harbors. By 1977 there was a ten-month wait for unloading in Jeddah. The private sector, spurred by the government's incentive, was quick to invest in a number of large-scale industries. These were two asbestos cement pipe plants needed for water distribution, an air-conditioner factory, a very large aluminum extrusion factory, a number of furniture factories, all manner of huge prefabricated panels factories and precast concrete plants, certainly among the largest in the world, and cement plants. The private sector also invested in all types of small industry (such as plastic household goods). By 1982, the main bottlenecks had disappeared and growth could take place more smoothly. The main airports were fully operational, the roads were good and plentiful, telephones were available and working well, hotels had been built, and airlines were serving the kingdom adequately.

Altogether, the industrialization of Saudi Arabia was underway. The government directly took responsibility for the development of the petrochemical industries and provided the necessary incentives to the private sector to meet the demand for all other goods in the kingdom, provided it fitted within the overall development plan.

It appears that King Faysal, helped by Prince Fahad, saw very early the potential of the kingdom, but also realized that the kingdom is not made of one homogeneous population. The wealth of the kingdom could be used to unify the kingdom under what would be perceived as the beneficence of the Saudis. The kingdom has 7 million citizens. The southwestern part may number over 1.5 million people, mostly of Yemeni blood. The cities of Jeddah, Holy Mecca, and Medina, due to the pilgrimage, have populations of mixed origin totalling close to 2 million. The eastern region has 1.2 million people, of which a Shi'a population, centered in Qatif, may number up to 500,000. Riyadh and Buraida, the main cities in Najd, were oases where the beduin population did not always live in good harmony with the desert beduin. The settled population in Riyadh and Qassim totals 1.8 million.[9] To consolidate the power of the Saudis it was important to see that wealth was distributed so as to please the largest number of people, and also to keep the King in control. Industrialization had the advantage of combining the two requirements. By being the sole source of the licenses needed to start potentially very profitable plants and operations and by controlling where and how subsidies were given, the central government and hence the King could be seen as the real and ultimate power instead of the traditional sheikhs.

The Kuwaiti government did not follow the Saudi pattern and

instead emphasized financial services and foreign investments. It is quite typical that the Industrial Bank originally created to support local industries in fact became involved in international lending. The bank was founded in 1973 as a joint venture between the ministry of finance, the Central Bank and 13 private institutions. The capital was KD 10 million. The interest rate to be charged to industries was 4 per cent. The bank, unlike SIDF in Saudi, was run like a regular commercial bank. It borrowed not only from the government but also from the local and international markets to fund its operations. By 1978:

> emphasis was placed on refining the Bank's investment and operating policies and fostering banking relationships in the Gulf area and internationally rather than on growth . . . [the bank's] investment portfolio witnessed a modest rate of growth, reflecting the management's reluctance to acquire assets at relatively low margins.[10]

In other words, the Industrial Bank preferred to lend outside Kuwait at good international rates rather than finance risky industrial projects in Kuwait itself at 4 per cent. The bank was managed like a regular financial institution whose main purpose is not to foster the industrialization of the country but to manage its assets as well as possible. In its annual report of 1978 quoted by Asa'ad in *Doing business in Kuwait*, the Industrial Bank says it had financed 114 projects for a total of KD 90 million. Although the bank was and still is of importance to the development of Kuwait it does not show a great deal of commitment by the government to fostering a quick industrialization. However it does point out that industrial development was viewed as a positive occurrence, but that it should happen in normal, i.e. market-related, circumstances.

As early as 1966 the government had set up a system of 'joint sector industries' in which the government would join forces with the private sector to develop industries. These new ventures were able to borrow up to KD 50 million from the government at 3 per cent.[11] These joint sector companies appear however not to have been directly involved in industrialization. The best known of these companies are KFTCIC and KIC, who are now major players in international finance. Until 1982, when KFTCIC and KIC were told to give some support to large borrowers in trouble because of the stock market crash, the two Ks had most of their activities overseas, as bond underwriters and syndication leaders. As in the case of the Industrial Bank it appears that the means of industrialization were somewhat sidestepped and changed into purely financial vehicles.

The population of Kuwait is only 1.7 million of which 60 per cent is expatriate.[12] The land surface is small (18,000 square kilometers). The Kuwaiti population is mostly of Uneiza origin, a tribe from Najd in Saudi Arabia. There is also a large minority of Palestinian origin. The population is mostly concentrated in or near Kuwait City. Unlike Saudi Arabia, homogeneity does not need to be as much of a concern to the ruling family. Kuwait could not have the ambition to become a world power. It has neither the human resources nor the land surface to think of developing into a large industrial power. Hence, to use its capital, it became a necessity for Kuwait to look outward. Through various investment companies, such as the Kuwait Investment Organization in London, the government became a major investor in the stable Western economies. The government earmarks every year 10 per cent of its budget for investments for 'future generations'. In 1983/4 KD 318.9 million and in 1984/5 KD 322.7 million were placed in the Reserve For Future Generations. In fiscal 1985/6 the RFFG was expected to receive KD 311.6 million.[13] The RFFG places its funds in other government-controlled companies which themselves invest in various financial instruments and equity in western corporations. Kuwait has bought stakes in Mercedes-Benz, Mannesman, 100 per cent of Santa-Fe, Gulf Oil's distribution channels in Europe, large amounts in shares on the stock markets of the US, Europe, and Japan.

By and large the foreign investment policy was extremely successful. Indeed by 1984, revenues from foreign investments were estimated to be between KD 1.4 and KD 1.6 billion per annum[14] and increasing along with the yearly increases of the RFFG of close to KD 325 million mentioned above. Revenues from oil and gas in fiscal 1984/5 were KD 2.9 billion and with the current decrease in prices of petroleum crude and refined products one can expect the investment income to become higher than the income from oil in a few years.

Kuwait, like all the other Gulf states, also passed on to its citizens the benefits of its oil revenues by providing free medical care, subsidized food prices, and all kinds of social benefits. However it also developed a practice of buying lands at very inflated values, thereby providing owners with great capital gains. From time to time lands that were not usable by the state for roads, the airport, etc. were sold off at low prices, to be eventually bought back at higher prices.

Table 1.1: Government spending on land purchases

Fiscal year	KD million	per cent current spending
1978/9	107.4	10.0
1979/80	263.9	18.0
1980/1	391.8	22.4
1981/2	444.2	22.3
1982/3	219.9	9.9
1983/4	227.3	10.8
1984/5	98.6	5.0

Source: *MEES,* vol. 29, no. 5, 11 November 1985, p. B1.

In a country of only 1.7 million inhabitants, these inflows which totalled US$ 6 billion in 7 years spurred the economy tremendously. Furthermore, there were very large infrastructure works undertaken by the government: new refineries, new roads, new airport, bigger harbor, housing, etc. The money supply in Kuwait shot up from KD 636 million in 1978 to 1,248 million in 1982.[15] Large pools of funds were available for investments. The government, having encouraged the creation of stock companies, encouraged also the buying and selling of shares in the local joint stock companies. Trading in shares became very quickly a major activity among Kuwaiti merchants and businessmen. An official stock exchange was opened in April 1977. In December 1977, the share prices suffered a setback due to the large number of issues brought to the market. The government intervened and bought all the shares necessary to stop prices from falling.[16] Thus assured that the government would protect share investments, the Kuwaitis became avid speculators. Later, to cope with the non-Kuwaiti share issues, a separate unofficial stock market, the famous Souk Al Manakh was opened. These two markets and their developments are reviewed in Chapter 4.

The State of Bahrain also profited from the oil boom, but in a lesser way. The production of petroleum in Bahrain which commenced in 1932 has been declining since 1970. Most of the petroleum produced comes from the off-shore Abu Safah field which is shared with Saudi Arabia. Production in 1976 was 45,000 barrels per day compared with 2 million for Kuwait and 8 million for Saudi. Bahrain has about 20 more years of production available in oil reserves. Hence it is vital for Bahrain to diversify its sources of income.

Traditionally Bahrain has been a haven for the people from Iran and the Arabian peninsula escaping persecution of one form or the other. Thus, Bahrain has become a mosaic of peoples which its population size does not reflect. The 1981 census showed 350,798 inhabitants of whom 32 per cent were foreign.[17] The local population of 240,000 comprises Sunni Arabs (including the royal family), Sunni Iranians, Shi'a Arabs, Shi'a Iranians, a large indigenous Shi'a population, a few Jewish and Bahai families. The foreigners include mainly large groups of Indians from Kerala and Goa, Pakistanis, 10,000 to 12,000 British, and smaller communities of Japanese, Americans, French and other nationalities.

Having little capital to invest in massive industrialization, the government had to find its niche in the Arabian Gulf. Its purpose was to develop an economy somewhat independent from local petroleum production, and able to support a quickly growing population. The 1981 census, quoted by the Arab Banking Corporation in its presentation on Bahrain, showed that 41.2 per cent of the Bahraini population was under 15 years of age. The government started a few large industrial projects which have created employment but which by themselves are not enough to take the growth in employable persons. The two main activities were the aluminum smelter (ALBA) and the Arab Shipbuilding and Repair Yard Company (ASRY).

ALBA was designed to take advantage of the cheap energy available in Bahrain and has been a success. The company is profitable, and has increased capacity and production. In fact in 1984 the Saudi government cancelled the plan it had to build a similar plant in Jubail and took a share participation in ALBA.

ASRY was designed to service the oil tankers that went to load in Kuwait and Ras Tanura in Saudi. The dry dock can take tankers of up to 200,000 tons. The company has been relatively successful in the sense that the dry dock and repair facilities have been used at near capacity. However, after eleven years of activity, it has still to show a profit. The market for this activity is suffering from overcapacity, and extreme competition from France, Portugal and even Dubai where a similar operation has been open for five years.

Bahrain has also attracted an iron pellet plant which started production in 1985 and a petrochemical plant is under construction. A large aluminum rolling mill of 40,000 tons capacity owned by the Gulf Cooperation Council members was completed and commissioned in February 1986.[18]

In 1975 Lebanon, which traditionally had been the provider of services to the whole peninsula, was effectively shut down by the civil war. That same year the government decided to start an Off-shore Banking Unit Sector. It was perceived that the banking services provided to the foreign and local companies in all the countries of the

Gulf were very poor. Hence it made sense to attract highly professional bankers and banks to use Bahrain as a base to service customers in the region and take advantage of the Lebanese debacle. These bankers became known as the suitcase bankers, flying off to Saudi, Kuwait and the Emirates to bring loans and take deposits. The system was very successful and created 4,000 jobs in banking, of which 2,500 went to Bahrainis, and a larger number in the services related to banking, such as computers, law services, office building, furniture, printing, etc.

Commercial Law was also adapted to start servicing companies. These firms were exempted from the traditional and expensive requirement of the Gulf countries to have a local sponsor, or local ownership. A number of consulting firms, maintenance companies and a major insurance company took advantage of the exempt status which also created the employment of Bahrainis. The banking laws and the law on exempt companies were merged to allow the creation of Bahraini-registered banks doing solely off-shore business, and with mixed Gulf ownership. This development gave birth to five banks owned by private individuals with combined assets of US$ 6 billion. The private shareholders of the exempt banks were from all the GCC countries, but the driving forces behind them were mostly Kuwaiti businessmen.

Bahrain also became the base for inter-Arab ventures. Gulf International Bank started in 1976 as a venture between SAMA, Bahrain, the Emirates and Kuwait. The Arab Banking Corporation capitalized at US$ 1 billion was formed by the governments of Libya, Iraq and Kuwait. In 1984 their total assets were US$ 18.5 billion.

To remain as the service center of the region Bahrain has to be sure to obtain easy access to all the countries around, and to maintain its ability to compete against the local businesses in Saudi Arabia, Kuwait, etc. Of course the main market in the region has been, and will remain, Saudi Arabia. It was therefore natural for the Bahrainis to actively support the Saudi efforts to start the Gulf Cooperation Council, and the building of a causeway between Al Khobar in Saudi and Bahrain.

NOTES

1. *Middle East Economic Digest*, London, 9 November 1973.
2. Saudi Arabian Monetary Agency, *Annual report*, 1401, p. 9.
3. Saudi Arabian Monetary Agency, *Annual report*, 1401, p. 174, and 1404, p. 192.

4. Rodney Wilson, *Banking and finance in the Arab Middle East*, Macmillan, London, 1983.

5. *Middle East Economic Digest*, London, 28 September 1972.

6. Ibid.

7. Maurice Fougerouse, *Bahrein, l'instant perdu*, Paris, 1983, p. 105.

8. Industrial Studies and Development Center, *Guide to industrial investments in Saudi Arabia*, 4th edition, Riyadh, 1975, p. 15.

9. These figures, except those concerning the Shi'a population, which were estimated in Bahrain, were computed from maps in Husain Hamza Bindagi, *Atlas of Saudi Arabia*, Oxford University Press, 1978.

10. Yunis Asa'ad, *The legal and practical guide to doing business in Kuwait*, vol. 3, Kuwait, 1979, pp. 112, 113.

11. Ibid, vol. 1.

12. *Middle East Economic Digest*, London, 28 September 1985.

13. *Middle East Economic Survey*, Nicosia, vol. 28, no. 47, and vol. 27, no. 48.

14. *Middle East Economic Survey*, Nicosia, vol. 27, no. 48, p. B2.

15. International Monetary Fund, *International financial statistics*, February 1986.

16. Yunis Asa'ad, *Doing business in Kuwait*, vol. 3, p. 12.

17. Arab Banking Corporation, *The Arab economies, structure and outlook*, Bahrain, 1983.

18. *Middle East Economic Survey*, Nicosia, vol. 29, no. 20, p. A13.

2

The Central Banks

In order to promote their policies the governments have created and used a number of institutions. Industrial policies were pushed by the industrial banks such as SIDF in Saudi Arabia and the Industrial Bank in Kuwait. Land policies were promoted by the Real Estate Bank in Saudi and in Kuwait. Agriculture was subsidized through the agricultural banks. The prominent institutions for the implementation of monetary policies were the central banks: the Saudi Arabian Monetary Agency, the Central Bank of Kuwait, and the Bahrain Monetary Agency. The amount of power wielded by these institutions is different in each of the three countries, but by far the most powerful is the Saudi Arabian Monetary Agency.

SAMA's main duties are to implement monetary policy, issue currency, act as a clearing house, and create a list of acceptable banks for SAMA itself and for the other ministries to use. Finally SAMA is responsible for investing the reserves of the kingdom.

The monetary policy is enforced through the use of reserve requirements imposed on the bank deposits, and through the issuance of regulations to be implemented by the banks. The reserve requirements force the banks to place at SAMA 2 per cent of all their savings deposits, and 7 per cent of all the check account deposits. The placings at SAMA are interest free. If the total deposits received amounts to more than 15 times its capital and reserves, a bank must deposit interest free at SAMA 50 per cent of those deposits. This last rule is very conservative since, by comparison, the US banks are allowed a leverage of 22 to 1, the French banks 44 to 1 and Asian banks are sometimes up to 150 to 1.[1]

The regulations issued from time to time can affect local and international banks very substantially. SAMA pursues the goals set by Sheikh Aba Al Khail, which can be somewhat different from those of the banks in Saudi and abroad. Sheikh Aba Al Khail for example wished that the banks use their extremely large liquidity to finance the expansion of industry in Saudi. This goal is in line with the wish of the King to make Saudi a major industrial power. For their part, the banks are more worried about credit worthiness of projects than about the long-term picture of industry in the kingdom.

The minister of finance created the Saudi Industrial Development Fund in 1974, to help provide long-term money to industrialists. However most companies still require medium-term loans to cover their permanent needs of working capital and the difference between the cost of any project and the amounts lent by SIDF and the required 25 per cent capital base. The banks on the other hand are not eager to lend medium-term. The risks in Saudi are too high and the returns too low.

In one of his numerous speeches Sheikh Aba Al Khail asked the banks to lend more medium-term and lend more to smaller companies.[2] He mentioned the fact that Saudi banks keep SR 4 billion (US\$ 1.2 billion) in deposits at SAMA above and beyond the reserve requirements. Further, the Saudi banks keep in Bahrain close to SR 14 billion. These two figures point at the enormous unused liquidity. The bankers in turn feel that medium-term lending is risky. Indeed the securities offered by the borrowers are usually worthless. According to an interpretation of the Shari'a law which only came out in 1980, mortgages are not permissible, although they were until then. The defaulting borrowers usually find friendly ears in the courts. Interest debts are never accepted as bone fide debts by the Shari'a judges. It is this writer's experience that banks will never get satisfaction in the courts. Hence banks prefer to stick to very short-term facilities.

Compounding the problems for the Saudi banks is the intense competition. Profits are small, especially on the facilities to good creditors. Until two years ago some foreign banks were very eager to lend medium-term in Saudi as will be seen later. Faced with the choice of high-risk lending in Saudi at relatively low returns or placing their funds in foreign banks, the Saudi banks thought it best to lend to the foreign banks. Normal inter-bank rates averaged 10 to 12 per cent, and sometimes much more if professionally managed. The Saudi banks were themselves obtaining their money from the Saudi depositors at not more than 2 per cent. Consequently, faced with a choice of making 10 per cent with minimal risk and of making perhaps 11 per cent with very high risks on medium-term lending, the result was obvious.

As a consequence of the lack of interest in local lending by the banks, SAMA issued series of regulations to nudge the banks in the right direction. One such regulation, which created the most controversy, was issued in January 1983:

Circular to All Banks Operating in the Kingdom

The Agency have noticed the appearance, from time to time of some press releases and advertisements of syndicated Saudi Riyal loans and other facilities being arranged in the kingdom between local banks and with the participation of foreign banks. It is well known that all banking transactions in the kingdom are governed by the articles of the Banking Control Act and are subject to its requirements, and that the general policy of the agency does not encourage the participation of foreign banks in Saudi Riyal financing operations. Despite the fact that no restrictions are being currently imposed on loans and advances by local banks to residents as long as they remain within the requirements of the Banking Control Act, the agency wishes all banks working in the kingdom to observe the following:

1 — Local banks may not invite foreign banks to participate in any Saudi Riyal syndicated transactions before obtaining prior approval from the agency.

2 — Local banks may not participate in Saudi Riyal syndicated transactions that are being arranged outside the kingdom whether they are for residents or non-residents without obtaining prior approval from the Agency.

3 — Local banks may not participate in foreign currency syndicated transactions being arranged for non-residents without prior approval of the agency in accordance with our circular no . . .[3]

The SAMA regulation very clearly forbade the Saudi banks from participating in Saudi riyals syndications arranged by non-Saudi banks. It also stopped the Saudi banks from leading dollar syndications without prior approval from SAMA. This regulation created panic in the Bahraini market.

A large number of Saudi and foreign corporations working in Saudi Arabia receive payments in Saudi riyals and hence to avoid foreign exchange risks need to borrow in Saudi riyals. Until 1983, the various companies could borrow from any Saudi or foreign bank. However, since in many cases the amounts involved were very large, the banks would syndicate the risk. The foreign banks who were more experienced in organizing syndications would normally have one or more

17

Saudi bank as participant.

The role of a Saudi bank in a syndication arranged by a foreign bank was three-fold:

(1) The Saudi bank would be the agent of the syndicate in Saudi. It was felt by the foreign banks that the law in Saudi being very vague, a local entity would stand a better chance to obtain redress from the local court; or at least, that any pressure on the borrower would carry more weight if brought to bear by a Saudi entity.

(2) On the contracting business. which included very large performance bonds and advance payment guarantees, the number of banks authorized to issue the bonds was and still is limited by SAMA, and usually would have to be issued by one bank only. It was therefore simpler for the syndicates to have the local Saudi bank issue the guarantees and bonds, which allowed the banks to share the risks with non-SAMA-approved banks.

(3) The foreign banks were usually short of Saudi riyals, and having a Saudi bank in the syndicate gave moral support to the member banks in case funding became too difficult.

There had also been a number of syndications and loans arranged by foreign banks in Saudi riyals, but the use of which was not to fund Saudi-related business. For instance, a corporation could in principle borrow in riyals and repay the loan in riyals even though its income may be in dollars, deutschemarks or pounds. Between March 1977 and May 1978 five Saudi riyal bond issues were arranged by five banks for a total of SR 360 million, all for non-Saudi borrowers.[4] SAMA at that time had made it known privately to its main correspondents that it would not like to see a further development of this type of facility. The warning was sufficient to stop any further borrowings in riyals by non-Saudi entities.

This Eurocurrency type of financing is common for the very large international borrowers. However, SAMA always worried about Saudi riyals being used in such a fashion. Indeed, these loans in Saudi riyals correspond to a net outflow of the currency from the kingdom and hence bring about the creation of a Euroriyal market, which SAMA cannot readily control. Large overseas riyal deposits can be changed from one currency to another without limit, and swings in value and Euro-rates can be substantial.

The 1983 regulations demanding that the Saudi banks obtain approval before organizing dollar denominated syndications virtually took the Saudi banks out of the Eurodollar market syndication leadership, thereby avoiding a potential outflow of dollars from the kingdom without having to impose foreign exchange controls.

One of the purposes of the regulations was to force the Saudi banks to lend to Saudi companies. By limiting the riyals syndication by foreign banks, SAMA expected to decrease the demand for riyals by the foreign institutions. A decrease in foreign demand for the Saudi currency would render the Saudi banks flush with riyals and hence force them to use their balances to lend to the Saudi companies. Table 2.1 gives figures from a consolidated balance sheet of all Saudi commercial banks.

Table 2.1: A consolidated balance sheet of all Saudi commercial banks (SR million)

Year	1401	1402	1403	1404
Cash balances	9,703	11,760	9,418	9,306
Foreign assets	48,474	55,689	56,452	67,602
Loans and investments	43,148	50,535	56,201	59,315
Deposits	74,745	95,420	98,550	110,286
Total assets	106,376	125,976	129,135	146,132

Source: Saudi Arabian Monetary Agency, *Annual reports*.

In 1401 65 per cent of all commercial banks' deposits had been placed by the Saudi banks in foreign banks, mostly in Bahrain. This amount must have appeared too high to SAMA and to the government. Since the OBU banks in Bahrain were very active in the kingdom, there must have been a great demand from Saudi companies for banking facilities which were not provided by the Saudi institutions.

The discouraging effect of the monetary agency's regulation on foreign bank lending in Saudi had of course some of the desired effects. Incentives for the Saudi banks to lend in Saudi Arabia increased. To use their cash the Saudi institutions could not rely on the foreign banks to do the marketing and negotiation of loans. They could not lend riyals to overseas corporations or individuals. Hence to maintain profitability, they had to lend locally. By 1404 the amount of riyals placed overseas still showed an increase in real terms, but as a percentage of deposits from Saudi companies and individuals, foreign asset and total overseas placements went from the 65 per cent in 1401 mentioned above to 57 per cent in 1404.

To complete the effect of the regulation on syndications, SAMA started issuing non-negotiable certificates of deposit which the banks could resell to SAMA if they needed quick funds (these instruments are often called 'repos', for redepositing, but in discussion of this topic they have often been referred to as treasury bills). The first instruments were for 90 days and were sold on average at SR 500 million per week. Later a 180 days instrument was issued. These repos C/Ds were considered to be only of mediocre attraction to the banks as they could and still can obtain better rates, on short-term deposit in Bahrain. Nevertheless it did affect SR liquidity in Bahrain.

SAMA had a few problems in implementing its C/D program. In Saudi the issuance of these C/Ds could have been viewed as condoning interest payments by the government. The issue was sidestepped by limiting the buyers to the commercial banks, and, although it probably would be strongly denied by SAMA itself, by issuing the C/Ds on a discounted basis so that the actual percentage interest paid would not appear on the notes themselves. The issuance of such paper was of some concern to the foreign banks active in the Saudi riyals market. Indeed, until the notes were available the Saudi banks had no place to invest short-term balances except in foreign banks. These deposits were important to all the banks active in Saudi riyals lending, which were mostly banks in Bahrain. However the volume and the rate of the C/Ds issued were not sufficient to stop completely the outflow of riyals to Bahrain. It became one more way for the monetary agency to control the flow. It also gave SAMA a new instrument to use in the control of the money supply in Saudi. In May 1984 *Arab Banking and Finance* (p. 21) quoted a Saudi banker who estimated the outstanding amount of repos to be not more than SR 5.2 billion, i.e. not more than 5 per cent of total bank deposits.

At about the same time, rumors were spreading in the foreign banking community that the Saudi government would impose a 10 per cent withholding tax on all foreign bank profits on Saudi based business. The 10 per cent withholding tax had been on the books for over 15 years, but had never been enforced. Indeed it was a difficult issue, since no one could impose a withholding tax on interest earned when, legally speaking, under the Shari'a code, which *is* the law of Saudi, there is no interest. If courts do not recognize interest as existing, how could the government and SAMA impose a withholding tax on non-existent earnings? The issue was hotly debated in Bahrain. To the knowledge of the writer the tax was never demanded by the government from any bank or corporation. It could be that this rumor was started by the Saudi monetary authorities themselves. Certain auditors in Saudi (one of whom was a former minister of finance) first advised their clients to establish reserves for potential payments of the withholding tax on foreign loans. The tax problem was eventually taken up by the banks' legal counsels who in turn included clauses in loan agreements with their Saudi customers stating that the tax *could* be imposed and hence be payable by the borrower. This legal addition would often make borrowing from foreign banks unattractive. The withholding tax scare had the effect of reducing the efforts of certain foreign banks from lending in Saudi, and hence reduced the outflow of riyals from the Saudi banks.

The total loans within Saudi by Saudi banks increased after the SAMA regulations from SR 51 billion in 1981/2 to SR 61.3 billion in 1983/4. However most of the increase took place in short-term lending for commerce (SR 17.7 billion in 1981/2 to SR 25.7 billion in 1983/4). Lending to manufacturing stayed the same at SR 4.8 billion.[5]

The amounts of riyals held in foreign banks did remain very high, SR 67.6 billion in 1404 (1984). SAMA's efforts were admirable but not sufficient. Nevertheless all the above regulations and considerations give a good image of SAMA's modus operandi. On the one hand SAMA wants to keep close control on its currency, on the other hand the Saudi government, and the Saudi public, have been traditionally opposed to exchange controls and to controls on the flow of capital. Further, the existence of a large Bahrain financial market, a great deal of which is based on Saudi riyal deposits, is vital to the Bahraini economy. The Saudis cannot allow a whole sector of the Bahraini economy to suffer too much as it could create unrest on the island. It seems therefore that SAMA's regulations were meant to steer a medium course between the variables in existence. It limited the Saudi banks' involvement in SR syndication arranged from abroad, which in turn discouraged the foreign banks from going it alone. It would not completely forbid the foreign banks from lending riyals in Saudi, or the Saudi banks from lending riyals to those foreign banks, thereby leaving some activity to Bahrain. SAMA does not impose but nudges strongly.

To increase its control of the financial markets in Saudi in the late 1970s SAMA brought the foreign banks under Saudi ownership without nationalization. It simply requested the banks to increase their capital by 60 per cent, restricting this increase to small Saudi buyers. This increase satisfied most foreign banks since they were able to keep the control of management. In a booming economy with a larger capital base the foreign-Saudi banks were able to greatly increase their lending ability and their deposit base so that the great increase in profits by these banks allowed the foreign owners to receive in dividends an amount which was virtually unchanged or even increased. Citibank, the general policy of which is to never be in a minority position in any of its ventures, resisted the move to Saudi-ization but eventually buckled under, and became in Saudi the Saudi American Bank.

Eventually pressure was brought by SAMA on the foreign management to Saudi-ize personnel. Today the Saudi influence on the boards and on the management is very substantial. In some banks one can see officers who have been 'recommended' by SAMA.

In 1981, a famous bankruptcy (or rather insolvency, since there is no legal bankruptcy in the kingdom) took place in Dharan on the east coast of Saudi Arabia. Abdullah Saleh Rajhi became insolvent after having taken positions on gold and silver which lost him over US$ 300 million, most of which had been lent by a few foreign banks and local depositors. All the creditors turned to SAMA for help. SAMA, having no jurisdiction over the money changers, tried to organize a proper liquidation of assets and a repayment to at least the small creditors, which eventually took place in 1985. However the major lenders are still waiting for a settlement. After the Dharan Rajhi problem SAMA had a good case for requesting that money changers come under its control. The government eventually agreed, and in December 1981 the first regulations to put the money changers under the umbrella of SAMA were issued.

SAMA's other roles are the same as those of the other central banks in the world. SAMA issues the currency in circulation which stood at SR 30,035 million in bills and coins in 1402, SR 35,924 million in 1403, and SR 35,400 million in 1404.[6]

SAMA also acts as clearing house for the commercial banks. It has five centers in which the regional clearing take place: Jeddah, Riyadh, Dammam, Abha, and Buraida. In terms of volume, SAMA's main role is to invest the financial reserves of the kingdom. Unike other Arab states, SAMA has principally kept its investments in bank deposits and in treasury bills and bonds (see Table 2.3).

Table 2.2: Average daily clearing house figures

Year	1402	1403	1404
Number of items	225,400	266,660	299,300
SR (million)	112,500	136,866	158,258

Source: Saudi Arabian Monetary Agency, *Annual reports.*

Table 2.3: Summarized list of assets of SAMA (1399-1402) (all figures in SR million)

Year	1399	1400	1401	1402
Gold	756	756	756	756
Convertible FX	25,469	28,621	37,548	40,037
Cash on hand	1,610	2,246	2,623	3,174
Deposits with banks abroad	62,224	69,758	93,823	80,557
Investments in foreign bonds	113,376	178,459	346,009	318,360
Other	8,341	4,656	22,323	14,146

Source: Computed from SAMA, *Annual reports.*

The breakdown of the bonds and deposits by type of bonds and currency is not released by the monetary agency. However it has been speculated by bankers that, in spite of some diversification in yen and deutschemark securities, the bulk of the bonds are held in US short-term treasury bills. The deposits are held by a number of banks deemed acceptable by SAMA. SAMA does not publish the list of acceptable banks, but again educated guesses have been made by observers of the Saudi scene. A list was published by *Arab Banking and Finance* of London in August 1983, which seems to have been accepted as closest to SAMA reality. It showed that only 58 institutions were accredited to receive deposits; these included Bank of Tokyo, Sumitomo, the four largest Swiss banks, Banque de Paris, Commerzbank, etc. The largest deposits, however, are held in the London branches of a few very large American banks: mainly, Morgan Guaranty Trust, Citibank, Chase, and Bank of America.

SAMA also compiles and publishes another list of banks deemed acceptable by the various government ministries for issuance of performance bonds, advance payment guarantees, and bid bonds. This list is important to the foreign banks and contractors. If any given bank's name is on the SAMA list it allows the bank to issue its bonds and guarantees directly in favor of whatever ministry is signing a contract. The foreign bank is not obliged to have the bonds confirmed by a local Saudi bank, which saves time and money to the contractors. This rule, implemented in 1978, allowed for great competition to develop between the foreign banks and the Saudi banks. The immediate gain to the contractors was a sharp reduction of bonding fees, and securities required by the banks. This writer experienced declines from 1.5 per cent per annum with 15 per cent cash collateral interest-free deposits in 1978 to 0.5 per cent per annum bonding fee with 0 to 5 per cent interest-bearing cash collateral in 1984. On a US\$ 10 million bonding facility it reduced the profitability of the facility for banks from approximately \$330,000 per annum down to \$65,000 per annum. The decrease in banking cost allowed the contractors to increase their competitiveness, which was indeed reflected in lower prices to the Saudi government.

Until 1985 the banks in Saudi Arabia were left to use their own best judgement, or that of their auditors, to account for the bad and non-accruing loans. It has been rumored in the press that up to 25 per cent of the aggregate risk assets of the Saudi banks was non-performing.[7] Certainly Saudi Arabia has a major problem with difficult loans. This is partly due to the deep recession that has hit the Saudi economy since mid-1985. However, there is a very major legal weakness in the Saudi banking system which rewards those who decide not to pay. This problem is reviewed in detail in Chapter 8. In the light of these difficulties, and to improve the reality of banks' balance sheets, SAMA has issued instructions telling the banks to categorize their non-performing loans between loans past due for up to 6 months, up to a year, and over a year. SAMA has also set up a central liability system which allows SAMA and the banks to see how much any one problem customer owes to the whole market.

The Central Bank of Kuwait, like its Saudi equivalent, is in charge of issuing the currency, of clearing and of controlling the banks. Its role however is not so prominent when it comes to enforcing monetary policy or investment policies.

The objectives of the Central Bank of Kuwait are:

1. To exercise the privilege of the issue of currency on behalf of the state.
2. To endeavor to secure the stability of the Kuwaiti currency and its free convertibility into foreign currencies.
3. To endeavor to direct credit policy in such manner as to assist the social and economic progress and the growth of national income.
4. To control the banking system in the state of Kuwait.
5. To serve as banker to the government.
6. To render financial advice to the government.[8]

The Central Bank of Kuwait arranges clearing for the banks in Kuwait, and also manages a portion of Kuwait's reserves (see Table 2.4).

Table 2.4: The role of the Central Bank of Kuwait

		1981	1982	1983	1984
(a)	Average daily clearing house figures (KD million)	3,575	6,875	2,370	1,563
(b)	Kuwait's reserves managed by the Central Bank (US$ million, rounded)				
	Gold	113	110	108	104
	IMF position	518	577	767	777
	Foreign assets	4,127	5,968	5,272	4,746

Source: Computed from IMF, *International financial statistics*, February 1986.

Kuwait's investments abroad are not all handled by the Central Bank. The government sets aside 10 per cent of all its revenues from oil and other sources and places that amount in the Reserve for Future Generations (RFFG). For the 1984/5 fiscal year this amounted to KD 274 million (US$ 933 million).[9] These funds in turn are channelled to various investment organizations responsible for placing the reserves in profitable ventures and instruments.

In 1982 the government set up the Kuwait Investment Authority which supervises and has overall responsibility for the foreign investments of Kuwait.[10] Prior to the establishment of KIA the government channelled the funds through a number of organizations, the main one being the government-owned Kuwait Investment Office (KIO). KIO was established in London in 1966 to take equity participations, usually minority positions, in European and American corporations. KIO today manages about US$ 30 billion worth of investments,[11] such as stakes in the Royal Bank of Scotland (14.7 per cent), Lonrho (sterling £72 million), Trust House Forte, etc. The government also controls two investment companies, the Kuwait Foreign Trading Contracting and Investing Company and the Kuwait International Investment Company, and has 27 per cent of the Kuwait Investment Company. KFTCIC, KIIC and KIC, often called the three Ks, have been used by the government to buy shares in Kuwait and in the Western world. Other channels have also been used for foreign investments if not purely financial. For instance, the Kuwait Petroleum Company was responsible for the acquisition of Santa Fe International Corporation in the United States, a gas and oil engineering firm, and of the distribution network of Gulf Oil Corporation in Europe.

The total amount of investments abroad has been estimated to total between US$ 50 and 80 billion.[12] This program has been hugely successful. In fact, as has been mentioned earlier, the total revenue earned by the State of Kuwait from its overseas investments is nearing petroleum revenue. *MEED* estimates the revenue from foreign investment to average about KD 1,436 million per year (US$ 4.9 billion) compared with oil revenue in 1984/5 of KD 2,448 million (US$ 8.3 billion).

The institutions which have handled the investments abroad for the State of Kuwait have not restricted their activities just to investments; they have also acted as investment bankers, underwriting bond issues in various currencies, including very large issues in Kuwaiti dinars. Between 1968 and 1973 a total of KD 829 million worth of bonds and notes was issued in 105 different transactions, most of which took place between 1974 and 1979 (computed from a KIIC table in Mehran Nakhjavani, *The Arab banks and the international markets*, 1983). However, after the stock market problems in Kuwait the role of Kuwaiti dinars started to decline very substantially. The funds are just not there to finance any such issue. Further, the denomination of notes and bonds in any currency demands a large depth of available funds to have a secondary market which will make the paper attractive to a large pool of investors. In fact, the Kuwaiti dinar became somewhat restricted as early as 1979 when the Central Bank imposed restrictions on KD deposits outside Kuwait. These restrictions dried up the KD pool of funds which had been traded by the OBU banks in Bahrain, and thus dried up the availability of KD funding by the foreign institutions interested in KD holdings.

In 1982 the famous crash of the Souk Al Manakh produced a void in the financial sector. The banks became burdened with enormous bad debts and the economy came to a standstill. All turned to the Central Bank for guidance, which tried to help devise some plans to save the banking sector. Mr Abdel Wahab al Tammar, the Governor of the Bank, said:

> Underpinning the whole package is the fundamental policy that the government has undertaken to fully underwrite the safety of Kuwait's financial system. When this base is secure, all the other financial institutions can safely revolve around it — the banks themselves can ensure that other institutions are adequately financed.[13]

However, the Central Bank was faced with a very great problem. The aggregate capital of the Kuwaiti banks is estimated at KD 1.1 billion but the total bad debts resulting from the Souk Al Manakh is between KD 1.7 and 2.0 billion. The amounts lent by the banks to their directors was KD 276 million, and about the same amount was lent to relations of the directors.[14] The banks felt secured by a pledge on the bank shares owned by their directors. However these shares declined along with the rest of the market. The banks are thus in difficulty because if they take the right amount of provisions their profits and net worth will disappear and the shares will be worth even less. The Central Bank was thus forced to impose a set of rules on the accounting of bad debts which the banks had been unable to decide for themselves.

The Central Bank issued the following rules on provisions:[15]

— 10 per cent of all performing loans below KD 20,000
— 5 per cent on all fully secured performing loans
— 15 per cent on loans past due over 61 days
— 45 per cent on loans past due over 180 days
— 100 per cent on loans past due over 365 days.

The first two rules are really reserve requirements, protecting the banks against further problems arising from the crisis. The last three rules are very tough for the banks, as these provisions could wipe out their entire net worth. The Central Bank must have thought, along with the statement of its Governor quoted above, that a clean banking system, however lowly capitalized, is better than an artificially capitalized system. The clean-up, linked to a firm stand by the government that it will deposit more funds in the banks (*MEES*, vol. 29, no. 8, pp. B1-4), and strong nudging of the foreign banks by the Central Bank to maintain their deposits in Kuwaiti institutions will ensure that the banking system will remain intact through the resolution of the crisis.

The Central Bank did not wish to become a strong controller and administrator of the country's financial and monetary policy. It stumbled upon its present role of administrator of the banking system through the stock market crisis. The crisis however has shaken the country so much that one cannot expect the Central Bank to relinquish this newly discovered strength. In fact even the businessmen who normally shy from government controls have called through the Chamber of Commerce for the Central Bank to stop being only a rubber stamp for the ministry of finance and to become stronger and independent.[16]

The Kuwaiti approach to foreign investments further points out the major difference between the Saudi and the Kuwaiti policies on central banking. Where the Saudis have a very powerful central institution which slowly but surely is taking control of all aspects of the financial markets, the Kuwaitis have decentralized decision-making and privatized the approach to investments and controls. The Saudis, through SAMA, invest only in short-term foreign government securities and short-term deposits, whereas the Kuwaitis invest in much riskier businesses, oil, industry, shares and corporate bonds, through a number of different institutions. The difference is mainly due to two different visions by the two governments of what their future should be. The Saudis see themselves as a future major industrial power, for which they must keep ready cash to plow in the development of the planned industries. The Kuwaitis prefer to see themselves as a type of multinational holding company, whose role is to manage financial assets to provide income to its small local population.

Between the two large financial powers of Saudi and Kuwait, lies the smaller and relatively poorer Bahrain. The Bahrain Monetary Agency (BMA) is responsible for the issue of currency, the clearing of checks for the local banks, the control of the local banking sector, the control of the Off-shore Banking Units, the investment of the reserves and more generally for all the financial activities undertaken in Bahrain by both local and foreign companies.

The currency issued increased greatly in the 1970s reflecting the very important increase in economic activity in Bahrain. In 1971 all currency issued amounted to BD 22.866 million, increasing to BD 61 million in 1980. An even bigger growth was reflected in M1 (total of currency outstanding plus checking accounts) and M2 (M1 plus savings accounts and time deposits) which went respectively from BD 24.56 million and BD 73.13 million in 1971 to BD 290.36 million and BD 477.8 million in 1980.[17] At 31 December 1984 the outstanding currency amounted to BD 83.5 million (US$ 221.69 million), up 6.2 per cent from 31 December 1983.[18] BMA's other responsibility is to centralize the clearing of checks. In 1984 the agency cleared 1,719,420 checks, up 3.5 per cent from 1,657,257 in 1983.[19]

The foreign assets managed by BMA increased along with the value of petroleum after 1973. Reserves in foreign currency were BD 22 million in 1971 and increased rapidly to reach BD 342 million by 1980 (US$ 855 million). Of course compared with the reserves of Kuwait and Saudi Arabia these amounts are minimal. The Bahrainis were well aware that their position was weak in the Gulf. They felt they were dependent on oil and even more so on the good will of their neighbors. To survive as an independent nation the government of Bahrain evaluated its role in the region and tried to find what it could offer to become a respected and necessary player in the region. It was with such thought in mind that the monetary agency developed the concept of the Overseas Banking Units, and viewed its relationship with all the financial institutions.

Bahrain Monetary Agency has striven to attract as many reputable banks as possible to expand the overall market and therefore the role of Bahrain as a service center. With the help of its British advisers, mainly John Moore, a British bank official, now an executive director at Lloyds Bank International, BMA established the rules under which the OBU banks must work. The OBUs have no restrictions on leverage and maximum lending limits. They have to report to BMA monthly their exposure by country and, more generally, their balance sheet and income statement. Profits of OBUs are tax-free, even though there are yearly fees of approximately $25,000 to pay as well as the local social security tax on salaries of 11 per cent paid by the employers (in addition to the 7 per cent contributed by the employees),[20] and a rent tax on the offices and houses used by each bank. These amounts are altogether minimal for the average bank.

The OBUs are not permitted to do banking business with Bahraini entities. However, BMA has made and even encouraged exceptions to this rule when it comes to lending to Bahraini-based corporations such as the Arab Iron and Steel Corporation or the Gulf Petrochemical Company.

BMA tends to advise rather than direct. *MEED*'s financial editor, representing the feeling of the banking community, wrote on 25 January 1986: 'BMA has developed a good relationship with the banking community, establishing firm guidelines rather than hard and fast rules.' The monetary agency will work behind the scene to help solve some of the problems encountered by the banks in the Gulf. It encourages new developments in the market away from traditional commercial banking to more investment banking type business. Mr Abdullah Saif, Governor of BMA, commenting on the slowdown in the region, was quoted by the *Financial Times*, 22 July 1985:

There is still a good basic operation here, but the market is changing rapidly. Successful bank management must be innovative in extending the range and quality of services, making use of new technology, and finding new vehicles to facilitate the flow of funds between lenders and borrowers. And we, as a supervisory authority, have to look at the prudential requirements.

BMA has always discouraged brass plate operations, and is not a tax haven *à la* Netherland Antilles. Bahrain does not have any tax treaties with the European countries or the United States and until now this has not been of any consequence in the development of the local financial markets. However, as the Bahraini-based banks become more powerful, it would greatly help their expansion in the US and in Europe if such treaties were negotiated. At the present time the Bahraini-based organizations which want to do business in the US must open branches there or use complicated accounting routes through Europe and Antilles tax havens.

The purely Bahraini banks are more tightly controlled by the BMA because they hold the deposits of the local citizens. The monetary agency has reserve requirements on deposits of 5 per cent on Bahraini dinars and 1 per cent on foreign currency deposits. BMA at present also imposes lending limits 'amounting to 15 per cent of capital and reserves for loans to single borrowers and related entities and 30 per cent to a bank board of directors collectively'.[21]

The regulations on lending limits are, however, enforced with some understanding. It was mentioned in *MEES* on 17 September 1984 that 'the BMA is to adopt a very flexible approach to the application of the new guidelines, and does not intend to put unwarranted pressure on borrowers in a difficult business environment'. The regulations, however, were necessary as a result of the excesses of the Souk Al Manakh. Certain banks had lent very large amounts of money to their directors. Although usually secured by real estate in Kuwait, or even by post-dated checks, the loans became non-performing and in some cases had to be written off when the borrowers lost all their net worth on the stock market. The securities which had been offered turned out to be worth next to nothing since all the creditors were selling all their securities at the same time. The subtle approach by the BMA on the loans to directors was rendered necessary to avoid forcing the banks to write off large amounts which in some cases might have wiped out the capital of the institutions.

The BMA, like SAMA until recently and the Central Bank of Kuwait, had left the regulations on non-accruals and write-offs to the common sense of management. The OBUs follow the requirements of their own auditors which are normally based on the requirements of the home base. The American and European banks will stop accruing and add to provision for losses according to the standard rules of bank accounting. However the true profitability of the banks registered in the Gulf can be questioned as a number of bad loans have been accruing interest, i.e. showing income on the books, when the chances of recovery are nil. SAMA and the Central Bank of Kuwait have begun to issue some regulations on accruals of bad loans, and one can expect these rules to become more widely followed in all the countries of the Gulf and in Bahrain in particular.

Bahrain started in 1986 to require that banks do not pay dividends unless approved by the monetary agency. The agency has also tightened reporting requirements, demanding to be informed of any shareholder with more than 5 per cent of the shares in a bank, and that loans be shown by economic rather than only by geographical categories.[22] These requirements are not burdensome for the banks, but will provide enough information to BMA to trigger close monitoring if loans for shares purchases to investment companies increase too rapidly.

Until now, however, BMA has acted less like a regulatory agency than a development agency trying to get business to Bahrain. Their efforts have been hugely successful. Even with the difficult situation in the financial markets of the Gulf due to the decline in oil revenues, the impact of the Souk Al Manakh, and of the Iran-Iraq war, Bahrain still has 175 banks. There are 20 local banking units, 6 of which are majority Bahraini, and these control most of the local business. There are 74 OBUs, as of December 1985, of which 14 were locally incorporated with equity totaling over US$ 2.9 billion, the balance being representative offices of foreign banks. The total assets of the OBUs have been fluctuating between US$ 60 and 65 billion, of which 75 per cent are US$ assets.

CBK, SAMA and BMA interact with their financial markets differently. Gently but inexorably, SAMA is moving to control all the markets in Saudi to meet the policy requirements of a fairly centralized industrial development. On the other extreme the Central Bank of Kuwait became a controlling entity in spite of itself and only to avoid the total collapse of the financial systems after the crash of the Souk Al Manakh in 1982. For its part the Bahrain Monetary Agency acts as a development agency of its own; it has a role to play in making Bahrain a service center for the region, and acts accordingly. It cajoles the banks into working from Bahrain while making sure that it does not develop a tax haven/brass plate reputation, or run counter to the financial policies of its bigger neighbors too strongly.

NOTES

1. John Presley, 'The development of commercial banking in Saudi

Arabia', in *Arab banking and finance handbook*, Falcon, Bahrain, 1983, p. 138.

2. *Middle East Economic Digest*, 7 April 1985.

3. Translation made by and published in *Arab Banking and Finance*, London, March 1983.

4. Mehran Nakhjavani, *Arab banks and the international financial markets*, MEPEP, Nicosia, 1983, p. 67.

5. *Financial Times*, 'Special report on Saudi Arabia', April 1985.

6. Saudi Arabian Monetary Agency, *Annual Report*, 1404, p. 142.

7. *Middle East Economic Survey*, vol. 29, no. 7, p. B4.

8. Yunis Asa'ad, *Doing business in Kuwait*, Kuwait, 1979, vol. 3, p. 21.

9. *Middle East Economic Survey*, vol. 29, no. 7, p. B2.

10. *Middle East Economic Digest*, 14 December 1985, p. 4.

11. Ibid.

12. Arab Banking Corporation, *The Arab economies, structure and outlook*, Bahrain, 1983, p. 59; and *Middle East Economic Digest*, 14 December 1985.

13. *Middle East Economic Survey*, vol. 28, no. 8, pp. B1-4.

14. *Middle East Economic Digest*, 4 January 1986, pp. 8, 9, 10.

15. Ibid.

16. *Middle East Economic Survey*, vol. 29, No. 6, p. B3.

17. Bahrain Monetary Agency, *Statistical report*, 4th quarter 1985.

18. Bahrain Monetary Agency, *Annual report*, 1984, p. 33.

19. Ibid., p. 34.

20. *Financial Times*, 'Special survey on Bahrain', 8 May 1984.

21. *Financial Times*, 'Special survey on Bahrain', 22 July 1985, p. 15.

22. *Middle East Economic Digest*, 25 January 1986, pp. 6, 7.

3

The Commercial Banks

In 1986 the commercial banks are still the main component of the financial markets in the Arabian Gulf. The type of business done by the banks in Saudi Arabia, Kuwait and Bahrain is quite similar. The 196 banks in the area service the small depositors and borrowers, but their main lending activities, especially for the OBUs in Bahrain, are limited to a small pool of customers numbering not more than 200 corporations or large private companies. Of course, not all 196 banks are active but it appears, at least to the writer, that about 100 banks have some substantial activity. In Kuwait the commercial banks which have deposits from the public at large lent 59 per cent of their risk assets to only 202 customers.[1] In Bahrain, the 175 banks present did not deal with more than 100 customers outside Bahrain. In Saudi the major activities of the banks were also limited to a few very large trading families. Therefore the active banks competed enormously for a very limited group of names, but on these names competition was intense and during the height of the oil boom the amount of risk taken was quite impressive.

Like all banks anywhere, the banks in the Arab Gulf were and still are basically offering loans, letters of credit, guarantees, and management of deposits. However there are notable differences due to the laws and particularities of the region. Further, there is an anecdotal interest in recording the business patterns that took place at the height of the oil boom, and which are as much a lesson in finance as a lesson in human frailty when faced with mountains of money.

The traditional business of the banks in the Arabian Gulf was trade finance. Until 1975 the countries produced virtually nothing besides petroleum. Hence most of the goods to be consumed had to be imported, which was done by private citizens who developed into major trading families, some of whom eventually became industrialists.

The purchase of goods by these traders had to be arranged through the banks. Perhaps a quick reminder of the letter of credit cycle may refresh the reader's memory, help outline the risks incurred by the banks, and show the sources of the profits to the banks.

Let us take, for example, the import of General Motors cars into the kingdom of Saudi Arabia. Sheikh X writes to GM and orders 100 cars for a total cost of US$ 1 million. GM does not know of Sheikh X and hence will feel it is at risk to send 100 cars not knowing whether it will be paid. On the other hand Sheikh X does not want to pay until he is sure that the cars will be delivered in Jeddah. To ease the transactions GM will require that a US bank confirms (i.e. becomes legally responsible for) the payment. Sheikh X will ask a Saudi bank to confirm the payment to the US bank but only against a list of documents, usually the invoice, the bill of lading, and a draft for the amount of the transaction. The Saudi bank then writes a letter to the US bank stating that the US bank can pay the exporter the value stated on the draft upon receipt by the US bank of the bill of lading, the invoice, insurance certificates and whatever other documents are required by Sheikh X. This sequence in the letter of credit cycle is called the negotiation of documents. The US bank willingly accepts such an order from the Saudi bank if they have a good and long-standing relationship. We will assume, and this assumption corresponds to the normal reality of business, that the US bank has substantial deposits from the Saudi bank. Upon receipt of the letter of credit from the Saudi bank, the US bank passes it on and confirms the transaction to GM. GM then ships the cars and gives to the US bank the bill of lading, witnessing the shipment, and the other documents required. The US bank immediately pays GM and debits the account of the Saudi bank. The Saudi bank in turns debits the account of Sheikh X, or most likely will provide Sheikh X with a loan facility until the cars are sold and cash is generated by Sheikh X on the transaction.

This very standard transaction has been the bread and butter of banks in the Middle East for the past 40 years. The profits to the banks can be substantial. Normally the bank charges a fee on the opening of the letter of credit, which until 1978 could average 3 per cent per annum. The fee however is only the tip of the profit iceberg. The banks, even for the very best local customers, normally keep as security about 20 per cent of the amount on the transaction as cash collateral on which no interest is paid. As mentioned above, the bank usually provides the customer with a loan or overdraft facility on which it charges interest at normal market rates. In Saudi in 1978 this was about 8 per cent per annum. The banks were paid by the customers in Saudi riyals and paid out US dollars, hence they also made a profit on the foreign exchange transaction. On a one million dollars import the profit to the bank would have been: 3 month fee on the letter of credit, i.e. US$ 7,500; interest spread on the loan of US$ 1 million minus the security deposit of US$ 200,000 for, say, 6 months at 8 per cent minus cost of funds at 2 per cent, i.e. US$ 24,000; profit on the foreign exchange transaction US$ 1,000; and profit on the interest-free cash collateral, i.e. US$ 6,000. Hence on a one million dollars transaction a bank could make US$ 38,500 within 6 months, a return of almost 8 per cent per annum. The average leverage of banks in Saudi Arabia being 18 to 1, this could have theoretically provided the banks with a return on capital of up to 146 per cent per annum.

The profits are excellent by any standards, however risks are not necessarily small. In the transaction described above, the bank is at risk with the buyer, Sheikh X. If the documents presented by the US bank are in proper order the Saudi bank is legally bound to pay. At that time the bank is out of pocket until repaid by the Saudi buyer. If the Saudi buyer goes bankrupt, or if only he is of bad faith, the bank will find it very hard to get repaid. In most countries the courts will force the buyer to pay or add the bank to a list of creditors in a bankruptcy proceeding, or will give the title to the goods to the bank. In Saudi however, there is no binding bankruptcy law; the goods will never be allocated to the bank as it would be tantamount to a mortgage on moveable property which is against the Shari'a law, at least as interpreted in Saudi. The interest charged by the banks on loans is never accepted in the courts as money owed because of the Shari'a law forbidding interest. Hence the bank is really lending totally unsecured and must know its customers very well.

Prior to the efforts of government, especially in Saudi Arabia, to get good financial reporting by the commercial and industrial establishment, financial analysis was either impossible or totally unreliable. Consequently the banks had to rely on the very old fashioned tools of credit review: reputation, family wealth, large deposits, etc. Banks were very much encouraged therefore to lend only to the rich, and not much or often at that. Profits were large on each transaction, but transactions were few. This situation was bound to attract slightly more aggressive bank policies, especially after 1973 when the demand for goods increased sharply.

Saudi imports by the private sector, which are normally channelled through the banks, increased from SR 4.7 billion in 1972 to SR 32.6 billion in 1980 and SR 61.3 billion in 1984.[2] The local banks were totally unable to cope with such growth, and the monetary agency was not willing or able to allow foreign banks to open in Saudi. Bahrain was quick to see the need for an off-shore banking system which could service the needs of importers in Saudi Arabia as well as in Kuwait. After 1975 the large international banks developed marketing teams based in Bahrain which would travel to all the countries of the Gulf to obtain business from the local importers. They were most successful where the need was highest — in Saudi. To open the letters of credit the banks arranged with their customers a system of codes used normally between banks called 'tested telexes'. These codes allow the bank to take irrevocable orders from its customers over the telex lines. The exchange of documents was done through the use of private couriers (the main one is DHL of California) who were able to have documents sent anywhere in the Gulf in less than two days.

The amounts of trade channelled through Bahrain are very hard to estimate as there are no breakdowns of off-balance sheet items, but an approximation can be deduced from the various official publications. Total imports financed by commercial banks in 1400 (1979–80) was SR 46.7 billion. Total private imports in Saudi was for the same year SR 100.3 billion.[3] With almost all trade transactions with the kingdom being handled through banks one can deduce that the balance between trade financed by the Saudi banks and the total imports was mainly arranged by Bahraini based banks, a volume of over US$ 18 billion.

The influence of Bahrain on the Saudi banks was very much felt. The rates charged went down considerably, often quite below the maximum rates imposed by SAMA in September 1979, and the banks became less conservative in opening their credits. It also forced them to modernize their operations to provide a better service to their customers.

Certain foreign banks based in Bahrain specialized in short-term facilities to precious metal dealers. Usually this activity was linked to purchases of metal by the money changers in the region, mostly those in Jeddah. These purchases involved real purchases with exchange of metal against money. To this effect certain banks, mostly two of the three largest Swiss banks, stored sizeable amounts of gold in Bahrain and Dubai, and arranged for delivery to the money changers in Bahrain, Kuwait and Saudi. They also sold to jewellers and individuals. This activity is highly specialized. It requires intimate knowledge of the gold markets, and well organized security and distribution systems, which only the Swiss banks have been able to develop over many years.

A few banks got involved in lending on precious metal paper purchases. This type of activity is common among the money changers. This is quite similar to a fully secured type of short-term loan. After all, the risk is only on the ability of the borrower to repay the amount which can be potentially lost over the period of the contract, since the bank keeps title to the precious metal until paid by the borrower. However, certain banks were more aggressive and started to lend on the margin.

Abdullah Saleh Al Rajhi, a money changer in Dammam, and the oldest son of Saleh Al Rajhi the biggest of all the money changers in the Gulf area, became a very active buyer of gold on the margin. Unfortunately, when the price of gold declined from US$ 800 an ounce to US$ 350 the banks asked him to cover his paper losses so that the difference between what he had borrowed and what he owned would be covered. Abdullah Saleh Al Rajhi was unable to cover the loss and went into liquidation. SAMA intervened to protect the small depositors of the establishment, but the banks are still trying to obtain some payments. A well-known Belgian bank is still short of an estimated US$ 180 million and its chances of getting anything back are remote.

In a case like the Al Rajhi bankruptcy, it is hard not to blame the banks. Certainly they felt confident that the oldest son of the largest and best known of all the money changers would be supported by his father, which did not happen. They had encouraged runaway speculation hoping to make substantial fees and interest for themselves in the process. The banks make money on each contract sold, often up to 2 per cent, and earn interest on the loans covering the purchases. A more thorough knowledge of the Rajhi family should have been a prerequisite for the Belgian bank before getting as exposed as they had. In other words an intimate knowledge of the market is an absolute necessity before large exposures are undertaken by the lenders. In the booming market of the late 1970s and early 1980s greed often overcame common sense.

Another product which was traditional in the Gulf banks was the issuance of bid bonds, performance bonds and advance payment guarantees. The government rules required the contractors bidding for any non-defense project to attach to their closed bids a bid bond for 1 per cent of the face value of the bid. Should the bid be successful the contractor would be required to provide a 5 per cent performance bond to protect the government in case of malpractice by the contractor during the construction.

The government also offered to the contractor an advance payment (20 per cent until 1980, and since 1980 10 per cent of the value of the contract). The purpose of the advance payment was to allow the contractors to mobilize their resources — i.e. to hire the workers, fly them to Saudi, buy cement, build housing for the staff, etc. — to start work under the contract. To obtain the advance payment the contractor had to provide a guarantee from a bank stating that the amount advanced would be reimbursed at the government's discretion if it were unsatisfied with the work being performed. These advances were almost always required by the contractors, and hence they had to turn to the banks to issue the bonds and the guarantee. The sheer volume of bonds and guarantees issued since 1973 is staggering. Gross fixed investments including the oil sector totalled SR 798 billion between 1394/5 and 1403/4. On the very conservative side this implies that banks issued SR 120 billion worth of bonds and advances over those 10 years (approximately US$ 3.5 billion per year).[4] The income realized from these operations became one of the major sources of profit of the banks.

Although all the Saudi banks were entitled to issue bonds and guarantees in favor of the Saudi government, only a limited list of foreign banks was deemed acceptable by SAMA. The list increased with time, and in essence includes today the major banks in each of the countries in the world which deal with Saudi Arabia, as well as the banks in which SAMA has a stake, such as GIB in Bahrain, SIB in London and Banco Saudi Español.

The system of advance payment was always used and often abused. Advance payments were used to buy equipment, sometimes much more equipment than was really needed. Sometimes advance payments were used to build new villas for the contractors themselves. Some contractors would spend all of the advance prior even to mobilizing, and would live from advance payment to advance payment. A famous case in point was National Chemical Industries of Jeddah. NCI went into liquidation (in this case a euphemism for fraudulent bankruptcy) for having played the game too much. The general idea was for the contractor to put in a bid just low enough to get the deal but not so low that the contracting engineers would dismiss the bid as unrealistic. The contractor would then woo the banks to issue the bonds and guarantees. Competition among the banks being intense, this was not too difficult to arrange, especially around 1980. Once the advance payment had been received, the contractor would not use the funds to mobilize but instead borrow from the banks, and use the government advance to invest in other unrelated assets usually abroad. NCI at the end of its existence had SR 1.7 billion of contracts on hand, and had received an estimated SR 250 million in advance payments. About US$ 20 million are still unaccounted for, and the Chairman and founder of the company, Sheikh Mohammed Yahya Bedrawi, has disappeared.

The Saudi contractors were not the only ones to enjoy the benefits of a large free deposit from the government. It has been said by some bankers that the Korean companies would make more money on the advance payments than on the contracts themselves. The Korean contracting companies, which are famous in the Middle East for their reliability and high quality workmanship, are also famous for their disciplined labor, which is almost entirely Korean. In most cases the Korean firms were able to take a contract and bring in raw material and labor themselves, for which they would pay at home in wons. Hence their real dollar mobilizing expenditures were minimal. They could therefore take the money, transfer it to their headquarters in Seoul and invest the funds in high return instruments and/or in general corporate treasury. Such use of the funds would allow the Korean firms to take the contracts at a lower profit margin than the competition, making them formidable competitors in the bidding.

Another favorite use of the advance payments was the specialty of the Land Oil group of the Philippines. The group, which was a major world conglomerate, controlled contracting firms, medical management companies, harbor management companies, engineering firms, oil-drilling companies, etc., all based on cheap but technically advanced Filipino workmanship. Land Oil and its group of companies had about SR 10 billion worth of contracts in Saudi Arabia. The advance payments were transferred to the parent company which then placed the money in all manner of investments, such as real estate in Europe and the US, in shares, in gold, etc. The decision making on the investments was done by one man, Jo de Venezia. Land Oil is now in bankruptcy, de Venezia is no longer seen in the main financial centers, and the banks who had lent to the group are now struggling to finish the contracts undertaken in Saudi and to get some money out of the government of the Philippines which had guaranteed part of the loans. The total exposure of Western and Arab banks to Land Oil is estimated by the writer to have been close to US$ 80 million, and it is unlikely that they will recoup much of it.

In 1980, to stop the obvious misuse of advance payments by unscrupulous firms and to reduce temptation to others, the government changed the advance payment from 20 per cent to 10 per cent. This decrease was the main factor in the fall of NCI and Land Oil who could no longer mobilize on a first contract by using funds from a second contract. It cleaned up the contracting industry. It did not however decrease the overall business of the banks. Although the banks would issue smaller bonds, it also meant that many contracting firms asked for greater loans to mobilize. It did change the nature of the risk to the banks because instead of having guaranteed exposure the banks now had real cash out.

A consequence of the very large volume of facilities required was the development of syndications. Between April 1971 and June 1983 the leading Arab banks had organized US$ 29 billion of syndicated loans.[5] Not all the loans thus syndicated were for Arab borrowers. Al UBAF, ABC and GIB organized large syndications for Latin America, Eastern Europe and China. On the other hand banks like the Arab Bank Ltd arranged US$ 1.0 billion of loans and guarantees for one customer, Saudi Oger of Riyadh.[6]

The syndicated loans are mostly attractive to the bank that lead-manages the syndication as it is able to maximize its fee income from the arrangment fee, or the 'shave' which it keeps between the arrangement fee paid by the customer and that received by the participating banks. The arranging bank often gets a great deal of prestige. Indeed, competition between banks being intense world-wide, obtaining a mandate from a prime customer is envied by all. The banks vying for a mandate but failing to obtain it will often participate in the same syndication as mere manager. Fortunately, there are more banks willing to take shares in the syndicates than there are banks able to place the syndications. The smaller banks or those having only a limited presence in the area find it a convenient method of increasing their risk assets for a minimum of marketing efforts. It is also a good way for a bank new to the region or to any given customer to develop its knowledge at a minimum cost.

The Arab banks, being for the most part the last-born of the major world banks, have had to fight hard to obtain the mandates to arrange various facilities. In terms of numbers, Gulf International Bank and Arab Banking Corporation fared quite well. They did hire some of the best talents available in the UK markets and aggressively went after the main Eurodollar borrowers. Between 1977 and 1983 GIB lead-managed over $4.1 billion of syndicated facilities, and ABC, which was only created in 1980, managed US$ 3.39 billion worth. Unfortunately a large number of these facilities were arranged for Latin American nations who are presently unlikely to repay their debt. Of the above figures, GIB placed 15.8 per cent in Latin America, and ABC 36.7 per cent.[7] This market having dried up, these two banks in the mid-1980s seem to be more aggressive in arranging facilities for Eastern Europe. With hindsight, one can easily dispute the wisdom of having made these loans and even of continuing on a similar tack in a part of the world which has not been known for its faithfulness to its commitments since the beginning of this century. In their defence one must say that GIB and ABC have been no better nor worse than the sophisticated Western banks, which have even bigger exposures to the same problem countries. Until 1982 Latin America was subject to major marketing efforts by all the Western banks. It was normal that very large new Arab banks with large capital and good deposit bases should feel like showing their new-found abilities.

Prestige, however, is not the only reason for syndicating facilities. As was mentioned above, the idea is to spread the risks between a number of institutions. In fact a large number of facilities were syndicated between the smaller banks in Saudi, Kuwait and Bahrain without ever appearing in the press. The 'club deals', as these syndications are called, allowed the customers to accept slightly higher costs since the other banks involved would not be informed of the rates paid. It allowed the banks to provide quick response without the normal lengthy legal involvements and facility letters usually the mark of publicly announced syndications. Finally it was viewed by many as the best way to deal in the Saudi market. If there had not been any publicity made around the large syndications done for Saudi customers, SAMA probably would not have thought of the regulation which limited the riyal-syndicated facilities. Club deals were accepted by the Saudi authorities because there was no official notification to the markets that the deals had been done and hence it did not imply that SAMA could appear to lose its control over the flows of riyals and of the financial markets within Saudi Arabia. After the 1983 SAMA regulation club deals continued, although they then did not include Saudi banks. The amount of facilities thus arranged privately cannot be estimated precisely but is certainly in the billions of riyals.

Medium-term lending is another product which has been available in the Arabian peninsula. However the perception of the markets by the banks, the traditions in the market, and the legal problems faced by enforcements against defaulting borrowers, made these medium-term loans few and far between. Certain banks, mainly a large French bank and a large American bank, felt that the text of the guarantees (required by the Saudi ministries for all performance bonds and advance payment guarantees) which had been drafted by SAMA, was too tight, and left the Saudi authorities sole judge of the contractor's performance. Indeed, the text of the guarantees required payment on call by the ministries without need for proof. However, there has never been a capricious call on any guarantee. In fact, the government could be blamed for having given too many chances to the contractors, especially the Saudi ones, prior to calling any bonds. The fear of capricious calls made the two banks mentioned favor loans, even medium-term loans, to the kingdom's main traders. Overall, their attitude was a mistake. Citibank probably netted over US$200 million profits on bonds and related facilities over the past 15 years, with probably no payments ever demanded by the government or its agencies.

The insurance companies, a good source of medium- and long-term lending in the United States and in Europe, were not interested in the regional market, and placed their funds elsewhere. Some banks did however have a preference for medium-term loans. SIBC in Saudi Arabia was created for this purpose. The balance sheets of Saudi companies, like those of most other Arab firms, show that most borrowings are short-term. Credit analysts normally like to see that fixed assets are financed by either equity or long-term debt, more or less matching the life of the asset. The analysts also would like to see a certain portion of the usual working capital of a firm financed by medium-term facilities. The reason for these requirements is that companies can be thrown into bankruptcy if, for one reason or another, the short-term facilities are not renewed. Banks also like medium-term because they tend to be more profitable facilities than the short-term ones; and they involve less work for management, as profits can be expected without fearing that the companies will not renew the facilities or renegotiate the rates downwards every year.

These management and credit analysis concepts, however, were totally foreign to the region. They were also based on certain expectations concerning the legal systems, which were approached with a Western frame of mind in an area where commercial law was always subordinated to the Shari'a law.

Because of the nature of the facilities the medium-term lenders tend to like secured facilities better than unsecured ones. A bank will prefer to have recourse on the assets it is financing. If it is financing machinery, for example, it will want a lien on the same; if a factory, it will want a mortgage, etc. Even if, with prime borrowers, there are no legal links, there will be the comfort that a given asset will bring cash flow.

Another important factor is to be reasonably sure that the interest to be paid over a period of years will be forthcoming, and that if there are problems with the facility that interest will be partially, at least, added to the principal and obtained from the sale of the security. However, in Saudi Arabia the law applying to bank facilities was not clear and has seen changes in a whimsical fashion. In 1974 banks were able to obtain mortgages on properties, although at that time there had been no formal foreclosures. By 1980 it was made known that mortgages were deemed to be against the religious law. One of the major problems for financial institutions in Saudi is the fickleness of the law. Under King Faysal there was a commercial code which was based on Egyptian law — itself based on French commercial law. However the application of the commercial code was always subject to Shari'a law, which is applied in Saudi by Shari'a judges. It appears to a Western mind that by itself this could be not only workable but also desirable as it would ensure that the rulings made on modern techniques of banking would in fact get tailored to the needs and traditions of the country.

Unfortunately, lately there has been an element of uncertainty which renders reliance on the system very difficult. Indeed, it appears that the notion of precedents does not apply in Saudi. Further there is no well organized system of appeal. Hence any disputes having to do with banks or financial institutions are treated like a political football with the debtor emphasizing the fact that the bank he has borrowed from is an 'evil, interest charging bloodsucker' (from a conversation with a Saudi borrower). One judge's ruling in Jeddah will be based on his views alone and will not even consider the judgement of a court in Riyadh on a similar case. It appears also to an outsider that there is no effort whatsoever to establish a Shari'a-based commercial code that would apply to all in the kingdom, with a defined system of appeals, and a review of the judges to make sure that the courts looking at complex financial transactions are competent to discuss the issues at stake. There is also a problem of enforcement. In theory a judgement can be enforced by the police. However, in practice the police may or may not cooperate with even a Shari'a judgement.

In view of the risks taken by the banks and the fact that they cannot rely on a fair trial, they have limited their business to short-term facilities which they can cancel at any time, except for large syndicated loans to government-owned companies, where the banks view the risk as being ultimately the Saudi government.

SAMA, as was explained in the previous chapter, has tried to force the banks to invest their large deposits in the kingdom, but one can hardly blame the banks for keeping half of their assets in other financial institutions abroad where they know they can rely on the courts to give them back their loans plus interest. More on this subject will be said later, but suffice it to say that there will be little incentive for the banks to take more risk in the kingdom until the legal system is improved.

In Bahrain and Kuwait where the principal of secured lending is well established and has received many precedents, the banks extended numerous medium-term facilities to local industries and traders. The facilities were used to finance factories, machinery, permanent working capital needs of big importers, land development, and in Kuwait, under various pretexts, to purchase shares on the stock markets.

Between 1980 and 1983 there were a number of syndicated loans floated in Bahrain, to lend very substantial amounts to Kuwaiti traders, fully secured by shares and land both in Kuwait and in the Emirates. These loans were attractive to many banks because it gave them an inside knowledge and a good introduction to well known families in Kuwait with whom they then hoped to develop further relations separately. Further, these facilities were often quite profitable, and, being secured, were easy to sell to credit committees in head offices. Of course after the crash of the market in Kuwait, the values of the securities and lands declined to one-tenth of their value, making the security almost worthless. A number of banks thus suffered substantial losses from these facilities which of course has tended to steer all lenders in the direction of sticking to short-term lending even if secured.

In spite of all the problems, certain banks have become very involved with a policy of systematically marketing medium-term loans to the very best industrial ventures in Saudi. Although it is difficult to report the exact amounts lent by Citibank, it is certainly above the $100 million mark. If the approach of Citibank was that the blue chip companies in Saudi would always need banking facilities to meet their requirements for permanent inventory, machinery and the like, and hence had to keep their facilities current, it is very likely that they played it right. Citibank has the resources in the region to follow the customer, evaluate each of the markets they are in, and provide the continuous support necessary during the downturns in the economy. On the other hand the banks in Bahrain who have been involved with lesser known borrowers and who do not have the follow-up capacities of Citibank find themselves fighting in the Saudi courts with the results mentioned above.

Up to now we have reviewed the asset side of the banks' balance sheet. The other and less risky side is the deposit-taking activities, and the management of the funds thus raised.

The local Kuwaiti, Bahraini and Saudi banks have the role of gathering deposits from the public at large.If the figures for deposits are broken down to show time versus demand deposits they reveal a systematic difference of structure between Kuwait and Bahrain on the one hand and Saudi Arabia on the other.

Table 3.1: Total demand and time deposits in commercial banks (converted and presented in US$ million)

	1982	1983	1984	1985 (Sept)
Saudi Arabia	23,000	23,930	26,250	24,340
Kuwait	10,199	13,765	13,632	14,352
Bahrain	1,888	2,047	1,994	2,143

Source: IMF, *International financial statistics*, various issues.

Table 3.2: Time deposits as percentage of total deposits

	1982 %	1983 %	1984 %	1985 (Sept) %
Saudi Arabia	38	47	47	48
Kuwait	76	79	85	85
Bahrain*	72	77	79	78

*Note: Excluding deposits held in OBUs.
Source: IMF, *International financial statistics*, various issues.

Deposits in Saudi Arabia are held mostly in interest-free demand deposits. The Bahraini and Kuwait public are quite experienced in terms of dealing with the banks and therefore demand that the banks provide them with a return on their money at least close to what they could get in New York or London. In Saudi Arabia the level of sophistication is much lower; further, there is also a definite religious feeling against earning as well as paying interest. The low levels of interest paid by the Saudi banks and in general the small amounts of funds kept in interest-earning time deposits in the kingdom allow the banks to be extremely profitable. With the development of the economy the public has become more aware and the trend for more time deposits relative to demand deposits is definitely upwards. In 1978 the ratio was only 20 per cent time versus demand.

In fact the potential profit offered by the Saudi banks' deposits is one of the most important factors in the development of the financial markets in Bahrain, together with the lack of response by the Saudi banks to the government's nudges to finance the development of industry at home.

After the establishment of the first OBUs in Bahrain it became very convenient for the Saudi banks to place their riyal funds in Bahrain, in short-term deposits, even overnight. This allowed the Saudi banks to obtain the maximum return on their balances at minimum risk, and keep a very high liquidity. On the other hand the Saudi government was eager to protect the stability of the system and has striven to maintain good stability of the riyal/dollar relationship. In 1974 the exchange rate was 3.5 riyals to the dollar. In December 1985, it was 3.65, having gone as high as 3.31 at the time of a very weak dollar; the total spread between highest and lowest being about 10 per cent over a period of 7 years. When compared to the 50 per cent swings over 18-month periods on the yen/dollar or DM/dollar, it is obvious that the banks and their traders could count on minimal foreign exchange risks when dealing riyals/dollars.

Between 1975 and 1980 the interest rates paid by the Bahrain banks on the Saudi riyal varied between 4 per cent and 12 per cent, but mostly stayed below 8 per cent. On the other hand the interest paid on US dollar deposits and loans was up to 14 per cent. It then became the favorite trick of all the banks to borrow Saudi riyals from the Saudi banks, change the riyals spot against US dollars, and place the dollars for the duration of the riyal deposits. At maturity of the riyal deposit, i.e. when the Bahrain-based bank had to repay its Saudi counterpart, it would change its dollars back to riyals and reimburse the Saudi banks. The banks then could make a profit of up to 10 per cent per annum minus whatever re-evaluation or plus any devaluation of the riyal which may have taken place during the time they held the deposits. The transaction was so attractive that it can safely be said that most OBUs in Bahrain were founded on the idea of taking advantage of this boon. In 1978 an OBU of a large American bank made more than US$ 6 million in trading profits, mostly attributable to the dollar/riyal play.

The trading rooms of the OBUs were the hearts of the organizations. Most of the Saudi banks were directly or indirectly active players in this market. National Commercial Bank of Jeddah, the largest Saudi bank, was a very major player in the market through its affiliate the Saudi National Commercial Bank. The Riyadh Bank also was a major player through its own affiliate, the Gulf Riyadh Bank, a joint venture with Credit Lyonnais of France. Citibank, ABN, and Banque Indosuez were easily funded in riyals by their Saudi sister banks. All the other banks were able to borrow directly from the Saudi banks and other friendly banks in Bahrain.

The game could be played more or less riskily depending on the bank's feelings on gapping positions, and foreign exchange risks. At any rate the main profits of the OBUs came from treasury management. Over a period of years, however, a differentiation of rates occured. SAMA made sure that the Saudi riyal would not become too international by forbidding banks from lending riyals to non-Saudi corporations and customers. Hence the flow of funds would go: Saudi individuals, to Saudi banks, to Bahrain-based institutions, to other Bahrain-based institutions, and lent back to Saudi banks, and to Saudi corporations and individuals. The value of the Saudi riyal remained very stable as the riyals sold spot were always bought back by banks covering their positions or eventually by SAMA whose main receipts being in dollars could easily take back its own currency. As the value of the riyal remained stable the changes took place in the interest rates. Over the years the riyal went from 4 per cent per annum to being equal to or even at times slightly higher than the dollar rates.

In 1986 with the problems existing in the petroleum markets, there has been some pressure on the Saudi riyal with rumors of massive devaluation relative to the US dollar. Hence at the beginning of 1986, banks were borrowing riyals heavily in order to have debts in riyals, changing spots into US dollars and hence they could make a good profit on the day their riyal debt had to be repaid with riyals that would be brought at a much cheaper exchange rate. Due to the demand for riyals, interest rates became substantially higher than the dollar rates.

Like all central banks, SAMA supported its currency and threatened to take action against the speculators. SAMA does carry a lot of weight as it is a major depositor in all the important institutions; further, the Saudi riyal market, not being international, like the DM or the yen, its ultimate value is controlled by the monetary agency. The market is relatively narrow with the total amount of Saudi riyals in Bahrain totalling the equivalent of around US$ 12 to 15 billion,[8] which pales in the light of the perhaps US$ 1 trillion in Eurocurrencies available. SAMA could absorb all the riyals outstanding. Therefore, threats by SAMA do carry some weight, even though to a small extent there will always be room for some form of speculation for or against the riyal.

The total assets of the OBUs which include all the treasury

activities and the loans both in and out of the region grew very rapidly. Starting from zero in 1975/6, the OBUs flourished to reach US$ 3.2 billion in 1978, US$ 50.7 in 1981,[9] and US$ 64 billion in 1984.[10] In 1985, in spite of the recession in the Gulf they remained around US$ 60 billion,[11] a level at which they should stay in light of the development of the Bahrain and Saudi-based banks which match the decrease in activities of the foreign banks.

In view of the potential profits to be made both within and without the kingdom, the Saudi banks realized that they should try to obtain the maximum amount of deposits from the public at low or no interest and saw that except in the main cities there were no banking facilities. The foreign joint-venture banks, which had until their Saudi-ization been limited to two or three branches, became very aggressive in opening more branches in the main cities and also in all the small country centers such as Khamis Mushait or Buraida. The number of branches opened went from 140 in 1399 to 524 in 1404, which was reflected in an increase in deposits from SR 40,548 million in 1399, to SR 109,293 million in 1404.[12] The large numbers mentioned, however, were not reached totally without problems. Each branch unit requires staff that is familiar with the area in which the branch is open, and fluent in the banking procedures. Further, the added cost of managing each riyal deposited in far away small branches is much higher than the added profit made on the same riyal. Nevertheless the banks were able to drain the riyals held all over the country and increase their lending within the kingdom, and also increase their placements in Bahrain. In order to cope with some of the management problems created by the opening of numerous branches and also the pressures from SAMA to Saudi-ize their operations, the Saudi banks jointly created a banking training center, to improve the skills of their Saudi employees. This center was actually modelled after a similar organization in Bahrain, which was very successful.

Similar efforts to increase the number of branches were made in Bahrain and in Kuwait. Kuwait has 155 branches of commercial banks,[13] and Bahrain an estimated 50. The number of branches increased greatly after 1975 reflecting the move of population to new suburbs and cities which was followed by the banks, eager to protect their market share.

In both Kuwait and Bahrain, women are able to use the same banking premises as the men. Nevertheless, the Islamic financial institutions in these countries have set up separate counters and entrances for men and women. However, as is the case in other banks, the staff behind the counters include both men and women. In Saudi, on the other hand, it was almost unknown to see a woman in the banks at all, especially after 1978 when the King forbade the employment of women if they had to be in any form of contact with men even if very remote. On the other hand, under Qur'anic law, women are fully responsible for their own money which they can manage without having to refer to their husband. Hence certain Saudi women do have substantial net worth, which they find difficult to manage in Saudi, since they are neither allowed to have contact with males outside their immediate families, nor are they allowed to drive and in general to move about without some kind of chaperone. The restrictions on Saudi women, which really only became strong after King Faysal came to the throne, were not a major problem for the very wealthy women, who had travelled extensively in the past and continued to do so, as they could manage their affairs from Beirut, Paris or London. However for middle-class women, the protection rendered to them under the Holy Qur'an was somewhat moot, as they had to rely fully on some very close male relative to take care of their business. The idea came to some banks to maximize deposits through opening bank branches managed by and reserved for women.

The bank managements counted on three factors to make the banking for women work. The first has been mentioned and was the theoretical financial independence of women. The second was the fact that many women, whether wives of foreign workers, or Saudis trained abroad, would be eager to get out of the house, and work for low wages. The third was that they expected the Saudi and non-Saudi potential customers to feel that the branches reserved for women could become almost social clubs, where the women could get together and at the same time transact all their business.

The first branches for women were opened in Jeddah in 1979, by the National Commercial Bank, Saudi Cairo Bank and Bank Al-Jazira and in 1980 by the Saudi American Bank (ex-Citibank) and Saudi British Bank (ex-BBME). The writer was told by some of the local Saudi bank officials that banking for women was not the success they expected it to be. Probably no one really knows why, but some ideas can be put forward. Although there is some public transport, middle-class women are very dependent on their relatives for getting about. Hence to go to their bank branch they are at the mercy of their husband/father, who may or may not agree with their wife/daughter actually taking responsibility for her financial affairs. Perhaps too few women are educated enough to realize the benefits they can obtain from the banks; they may view them as foreign anti-Moslem institutions. Also the rich Saudi women use the foreign banks abroad, and do not patronize the local banks. Any of these suggestions or combination of them is probably behind the lack of success of women's branches.

Until now, the commercial banks have been the center of the financial markets in the region. As the recipients of most deposits, and lenders of most funds, they are directly affected by the changes in the economic situation in the region. The banks in each of the Gulf countries are under a high level of supervision by their central banks and the monetary authorities, hence their abilities to expand and diversify their activities are curtailed by political and social factors in which they have little say. Nevertheless, and in spite of the present recession in the Arabian Gulf, the banks still play a major role in the development of the economies, and will continue to do so for the foreseeable future. Of course, they are by no means the only components of the financial markets, but every type of financial institution at one point or another must operate through the commercial banks, whether they be local or international.

NOTES

1. *Middle East Economic Survey*, vol. 29, no. 8, p. B3.
2. Industrial Studies and Development Center, *Guide to industrial investment in Saudi Arabia*, 4th edn, Riyadh, 1975, p. 16, and Saudi Arabian Monetary Agency: *Annual report*, 1404, p. 175.
3. SAMA, *Annual report*, 1401, pp. 151, 152.
4. Estimated from SAMA, Annual reports, Table 6.5.
5. Mehran Nakhjavani, *Arab banks and the international financial markets*, MEPEP, Nicosia, 1983, p. 23.
6. Ibid., p. 40.
7. Ibid., pp. 32-3.
8. Bahrain Monetary Agency, *Annual report*, 1984, p. 26.
9. Alan Moore, 'Bahrain's offshore banking units', in *Arab Banking and Finance Handbook*, Falcon, Bahrain, 1983, p. 92.
10. Bahrain Monetary Agency, *Annual report*, p. 27.
11. *Financial Times*, 'Bahrain Survey', 22 July 1985, p. 5.
12. SAMA, *Annual reports*, 1401 and 1404.
13. Central Bank of Kuwait, *Economic chart book*, 1985, Kuwait, p. 23.

4

The Stock Markets

In response to the very quick development of the region after 1973, there was a tremendous demand for capital. The families that had made large amounts of money in trade were able to finance their new activities out of their profits; they were also able to start new ventures transferring funds from their main business. However for the very large projects or for the bright young people with ideas and energy it was very difficult to find the proper capital.

The Kuwaitis were the first to see the potential which existed in the old-fashioned capitalistic system of selling shares to the public, to raise enough money to get any company started. Their law facilitated the establishment of companies and allowed for shares to be created. Shares of capital stock once issued to the public could be bought and sold and hence the Kuwait stock market was born. The shares were traded as early as 1962, but there was no official exchange until 1977.

In Saudi Arabia the main source of funds was the government. The large projects like the petroleum-based industries in Jubail and Yanbo were actually capitalized by the government through direct inflow of capital or through the Public Investment Fund. PIF's role is to capitalize projects or corporations such as the airline, the bus companies, the petrochemical ventures, and eventually, once profitable, to sell the shares to the public at large to foster the interest of the whole nation in the industrial development of the kingdom. The corporation law in Saudi is non-conducive to a lively stock market. Any company which wishes to be established as a publicly-owned corporation with freely exchangeable shares must be registered through a decree from the King. Of course, requesting such a decree would put the founding members somewhat at the mercy of the King and his entourage. Hence very few private citizens have tried to obtain such a decree to found a publicly-held firm.

Most investors in Saudi found it more practical and faster to establish limited liability companies, where the founding members are few and where the shares cannot be sold without the approval of the other shareholders. Any sales in the shares of such companies are subject to lengthy negotiations between the existing and potential shareholders, and in fact such exchanges rarely take place.

The only publicly-held companies were started under the sponsorship of the government. The first company to sell shares to the public was the Saudi Arabian Fertilizer Company (SAFCO), a large fertilizer plant founded by the government with 'the participation of the private sector'.[1] Much later shares were offered to the public by the foreign banks which had been forced by the monetary agency to become Saudi entities. The sale of bank shares was strictly controlled. Each bank gave to SAMA a list of founding members who as a group were limited to take not more than 20 per cent of the total capitalization of the banks; no shareholder was allowed to own more than 5 per cent of the shares. The list of founding members had to be approved by SAMA, who had and exercised the right to veto some of the potential founding members' names. The list of founding members and the statutes of the new bank were published in the official gazette. The shares were then sold to the public for whom 40 per cent of the total capitalization was reserved. The percentages were very carefully computed to allow the foreign banks to feel that they could keep control of the management. It also allowed no individual or family to control any of the newly formed banks in the kingdom. Basically it allowed SAMA to have a strong say in the general direction of the banks as the monetary agency could rally and speak for the small shareholders.

The sale of the bank shares was vastly oversubscribed, showing that there were people holding a large pool of funds in the kingdom willing to place money in shares of firms which were basically considered evil by many of the conservative factions. A market started to develop for the shares. However the Ministry of Commerce and SAMA kept close control of these exchanges. SAMA demanded that the shares be registered by the bank themselves, so that no one could start monopolizing the shares. In September 1984 SAMA restricted the brokerage of such shares to the banks themselves. The banks were allowed to charge 1 per cent commission on the transaction. In order to facilitate the clearing and registration process, the banks got together and started a joint venture, the Saudi Share Registration Company, to handle all share transactions. The present system is not very satisfactory; it takes three weeks for the exchange of shares to be completed, and the price at which the transaction takes place is made without reference to a general market trend.[2]

The seven formerly foreign-owned banks are not the only publicly-held companies in Saudi. There are 21 companies in Saudi which are publicly owned with a total capital of SR 14.7 billion. They include such firms as the large electricity company SCECO, the bus company SAPTCO, and the company that owned most of the industries in Jubail and Yanbo, SABIC. Basically it includes all the companies sponsored by the government with the purpose of developing the kingdom. In January 1984, SABIC raised 2 billion riyals by selling shares to the public. The issue was largely oversubscribed. The Saudi government had set aside a portion of the shareholding for citizens of the Gulf Cooperation Council, but the sale of this portion was not successful.[3]

The electricity companies, which before 1978 were mostly very small, in the form of limited liability companies and owned by very diversified groups of investors, were forced to merge into major corporations. Again the public was used to dilute the large shareholders and allow the government to impose its control over the development of that activity. In truth, in the domain of electricity this was a blessing for the user, since large utility companies, all controlled by one ministry, were able to unify the type of current used in the kingdom, and to provide the very large investments needed to generate the growing need of the kingdom for power. The figures provide a good image of this development. In 1393 there were four types of voltage used on two types of cycles and consumption that year was 1,005 million kWh. In 1400, there was only one type of electricity and 17,597 million kWh generated,[4] with enough capacity in place for years to come.

To induce the public to participate in the development of the kingdom, the government went to great lengths to make shares attractive. In the case of the utilities and in the case of the bus company SAPTCO, the government guaranteed to investors a minimum return of 15 per cent per annum.[5] As a rule the companies were not very profitable especially in their start-up stages and consequently the dividends were often paid out of government subsidies. Ownership of shares guaranteed to return 15 per cent per annum is very attractive and should a free market for these shares develop the bidding would be fierce. The chances are that only a few rich families would end up owning them, making control by the government more difficult. Hence it is not likely that the government will allow any of these shares on an open market.

The development of an official stock exchange in the kingdom has been a leitmotif in the press for the last ten years. However, to this day the government has managed to eschew the creation of a real market. Shares are bought and sold with a few brokers in Jeddah, but this activity is not yet a market as such, especially since the bank shares now have to be traded through the banks themselves.

The delay by the government is not only due to the fear of losing control of the publicly-held companies to a few large groups as was mentioned earlier. It is also due to a genuine desire to involve a large segment of the population in the fruits of development. Finally, a very major fear was stirred by the Kuwaiti problems of the Souk Al Manakh. Just as SAMA has been suspicious of the Bahraini banks for fear of losing its grip on its own currency and monetary policy, the government has been wary of the large Gulf financiers. The Saudi government has a long-term and ambitious view of its own industrial development, and may well be afraid that the shares will be very attractive to the large share dealers in Kuwait. The shares, if bought directly or through stooges, could be bid up beyond control and render the whole share market of Saudi securities as volatile and risky as the Kuwaiti market was until 1982. There is undoubtedly a genuine concern to protect the public from the dangers of speculation.

The lack of a real exchange is hurting the development of the capital markets. Prices are not set according to trends or in an educated fashion, and the fact that sales of shares are lengthy hinders most investors. In 1985 the National Industrial Company, set up to found and capitalize the second generation of industries using the industrial outputs of Jubail and Yanbo, brought its shares to the market. The floating of these shares was not an overwhelming success, and was finalized only after various agencies of the government intervened to buy the outstanding offered shares. As a result, the floating of shares by other companies seems to have been postponed indefinitely. Undoubtedly the lack of enthusiasm for the new shares is partly due to the decrease in liquidity coming from the changes in the oil market. However, there are still very large deposits in the banks which could be invested in industrial and commercial ventures. It seems more likely that the low demand for shares from the public at large is due to fears that the shares will be traded in an unfair fashion in the absence of a real and open market.

All the government concerns and procedures point to a very conservative approach to capitalizing *à la* Kuwait. On the other hand it seems that the ministries of commerce and of finance do wish to pass on to the public some of the benefits of the general industrialization of the kingdom, as well as to foster an interest in this development. The industrialization has been the brainchild of the present King Fahad, since his days as adviser to King Faysal, and certainly he has been the key to the development of the present share exchange system. It appears that the government and the King do not wish to lose any of the control of large industrial projects while trying to foster great public support of the projects. It is both good for the country and the King to know that the citizens will have a financial interest in the projects which can only do well in a politically and socially stable environment. Further, the public will see that the bounties come from the King and hence will support him against other political alliances which may not view industrialization with the same positive outlook.

The concern to protect the public is also a major reason why there has been no official market created in Bahrain. The Bahraini public did take a minor part and by and large was taken advantage of during the days of the Souk Al Manakh. More will be said about this later in this chapter, but suffice to say that much money was lost by small investors to the Kuwaiti speculators. The government is also probably wary of losing control of a stock exchange to clever traders.

There are 21 local joint stock companies in Bahrain with BD 133 million in total capital, somewhat eclipsed by the 13 off-shore joint stock companies with total capital of BD 525 million.[6] The purely local companies tend to have large nominal values while the mostly Kuwaiti founders of off-shore companies had decided to have very low nominal values on the shares. The decision to have low values on the shares was to create a penny stock market that would attract the small shareholders, who then could bid up the prices easily.

All the publicly-held companies registered in Bahrain have capital from all over the Gulf. This activity increased with the development of the GCC since, because of its location and more liberal laws and traditions, Bahrain is the ideal place for the creation of Gulf companies. These companies however should have given rise to an active share market which should have become the source of capital for all manner of ventures in the region. However, the Souk Al Manakh has rendered everyone very cautious and the Bahrain government has delayed the opening of an official stock exchange. Further, the decline in petroleum prices of the 1980s has decreased the amount of funds available and the six-year-old Iran-Iraq war has made investors very wary of investing in the region.

The Souk Al Manakh has been mentioned over and over in this text, because it has had a major impact on the financial markets of the whole Arabian Pensinsula and Gulf, and will continue to do so for years to come. The crash took place in August 1982. Until the month of May share prices had been going up on both the official stock market and the Souk Al Manakh. The indexes of Gulf shares and of real estate companies went from approximately 500 in December 1981 to 1,050 in May 1982. The index of bank shares went from 300 in March 1980 to 950 in May 1982.[7] By the end of 1983 the market had almost disappeared, with no buyers available except the government and its investment companies. The market has continued to fall and declined a further 60 to 70 per cent between December 1983 and October 1985.[8]

The Souk Al Manakh (sometimes also called the 'parallel market') started in 1977 when the government began to regulate the exchange of shares in Kuwait. The regulations had become a necessity because of the continual boom-bust cycles of prices of the shares of publicly-held Kuwaiti companies. Kuwait had been the first Gulf country to feel the benefits of oil revenues. With its more open society, a production of 2 million barrels per day and a population of only 1 million, Kuwait became the richest country on earth on a per capita basis. As a consequence the citizenry had large amounts of cash and hence share prices were regularly bid up beyond economic sense. Eventually the price would crash as people became aware that the companies whose shares were being traded could not possibly generate the type of profits which would have provided a decent return on the purchase price.[9]

In 1963, 1973, 1975 and 1977 the government intervened to maintain the price of shares. The government decided in December 1977 to open an official stock exchange which it could monitor and thus hopefully avoid the boom-bust cycles. A few months after the opening of the official stock exchange:

> the government undertook to purchase any amount of shares offered for sale at the price prescribed by the government. This step was taken to fix a temporary minimum limit for share prices and to protect those prices from dropping to such levels which might jeopardize confidence in the market.[10]

In other words the government instructed KFTCIC and other government-controlled institutions to intervene in the market so that prices would not get depressed. The lesson, well learned by all, was that the Kuwaiti government would not let its citizens lose money on stock exchange plays.

However, to minimize speculation the government also issued rules enforcing the registration of forward dealings with the ministry of commerce. Dealings were restricted to the existing companies. The issuance of post-dated checks was forbidden. Further, to help the newly born official exchange absorb the outstanding shares of the listed companies, no new shareholding companies were allowed to be established, and no capital increases of the existing companies were permitted.

These restrictions were cumbersome for the speculators. There was still a great deal of liquidity in the market. Alternative investments were only available abroad, which is not always attractive to the average citizen, and many Kuwaitis felt they should maintain a certain freedom of action in Kuwait on shares. To get away from the government restrictions, but nevertheless quite sure from the previous rescues that the government would never let them down, a number of Kuwaitis started trading shares not listed in the official stock exchange. A parallel market developed on which investors bought and sold a whole group of new corporations. The new corporations were naturally founded outside Kuwait to by-pass the regulations at home.[11] The Kuwaiti businessmen were able to take advantage of the laws of the Emirates and of Bahrain allowing part ownership of locally registered companies by residents of other Gulf countries. This trend was increased with the development of the Gulf Cooperation Council, the aim of which is to unify all the countries in the area. The main companies were created in Bahrain and in the Emirates, and were usually investment companies and banks.

The parallel market was completely free from any control by the government. The market developed and fed on itself in a gold rush atmosphere. The first dealings took place in a shopping center in the middle of Kuwait city, called the Souk Al Manakh. Most speculators and share dealers opened shop in the market, and basically set up what amounted to a trading floor.

The volume of trade grew briskly, profits were quick, and many Kuwaitis became involved in the market. It was commonplace to hear the Kuwaitis saying they preferred to place their money in the stock exchanges of Kuwait as the returns they earned were much higher than any possible return in other countries. From 1977 to 1982, the stock exchanges of New York, and of Western Europe were in the doldrums, real estate returned less than 7 per cent, and the US dollar was very weak. Hence, high returns in Kuwaiti dinars, accompanied by what the investors felt was an underlying and unofficial guarantee from the government, made speculative investment in Kuwait very attractive and simple. *Arab Banking and Finance* of August 1983 wrote that 6,000 prominent people, most of Kuwait's 'Who's Who', were involved in the market. There were also unknown throngs of small investors up and down the Arabian Gulf. However, only a few (eight to ten) large financiers led the market. The creations of companies up and down the Gulf were their brainchildren. The concept was to develop all kinds of instruments with very low nominal value that could be bought easily even by the smallest savers and bid up to over triple their prices, at which point they could unload their shares at vast profits.

This scheme was typical of what happened with some of the Bahraini Exempt Companies, which were created by Kuwaiti investors in 1980/1. More precisely, a group of Kuwaiti investors would get together and create, say, a bank. They would capitalize the bank for a very large amount, say US$ 80 million, then would issue penny shares to raise an extra US$ 20 million in capital. It was important to choose a type of company which gave potential investors the impression that it would develop into a solid and long-term money maker. Hence, banks were high on the list, especially if they were founded with a very large capital which gave an enhanced feeling of security to the small shareholders.

Upon announcement of the founding of a company there would be a tremendous rush from investors from all over the Gulf to subscribe for the shares. If investors were able to obtain the shares at subscription time they would pay only the face value of the share, usually US$ 1.00, or BD 1.000 (US$ 2.50), and hope to make large gains immediately as the shares would probably be worth many times that amount on the Souk Al Manakh. In some cases prices on the Souk were bid up to 15 times their par value. In other cases the shares were even traded before the registration of the company was final and the shares actually printed. The potential investors were given a few days to register their subscription at the office of a local auditing firm, such as Talal Abu Ghazaleh, who also happened to be a major player in this market. At the time of actual subscription of the shares, potential buyers had to deposit 10 per cent of the value of the shares they wished to buy. In most cases, the shares were oversubscribed, sometimes by as much as 1,000 times. Eventually shares were issued as a percentage of the total subscribed. The rush for shares in 1981 was so strong that on several occasions the central banks in the region had to intervene to provide the banks with liquidity to help them face the withdrawal of deposits made by aspiring investors — just to cover the 10 per cent security deposits on the bids for shares strained the normally very liquid local commercial banks.

In most cases, the number of shares per investor was limited. To by-pass this regulation some Kuwaiti dealers would roam the villages of the Gulf countries and 'lease' peoples' passports. In order to register shares, investors had to present their passport on which was written the amount they wished to purchase upon final issuing of the shares. These modern carpetbaggers then were able to accumulate the shares by obtaining as many passports as possible and making their owners sign a power of attorney allowing the sale of shares upon issuance. Such canvassing techniques did indeed bring much attention to each issue of shares and almost guaranteed a vast oversubscription. The oversubscription was of course music to the ears of original founders since a 1,000 times oversubscription indicated an enormous share demand. The rumors of large demand satisfied potential investors that after issuance the share prices would be bid up very high, thus snowballing the subscription, as naturally the small investors felt that if demand was so staggering they would do well to rush to buy the shares at par when they could be sure that upon issuance they would likely go up three to fifteen times.

Eventually the actual shares were issued. Once distributed to the registered owner or his proxy the shares were traded. The oversubscription being such a well known fact, investors were satisfied that even if they had not obtained all the shares they wanted at the issue price they still could buy at the market price, which would be sure to increase in view of the demand for the share. The large Kuwaiti financiers who had put up the US$ 80 million, say, were then able to sell 20 per cent of their shares and recover their total investment plus major profits while retaining complete control of the companies they had created. Of course the companies created by these share issues did not have any activity at the time the shares were first traded and their prices were certainly not based on their bottom line profits, nor even on their expected profits. The economic viability of the firms was never a major factor in the share price, it was merely an excuse to play the markets.

The demand for shares on the Souk Al Manakh was artificially maintained. At the core of the Souk trade was the issuance of post-dated checks. The concept in this case is similar to that of buying on the margin except that the margin is 0 per cent. In other words, any buyer could buy a share at a given price, pay with a post-dated check dated for, say, 18 months from the transaction date, sell the shares the next day at a hefty profit and be paid similarly by a post-dated check 18 months from the new transaction date. These purchases could and did go to staggering heights as there was no money down and paper profits were enormous. Indeed the profits were even increased by the premiums charged on the checks which included interest on the money advanced and a premium for the opportunity cost of not having the cash on hand for buying more shares. Of course all the main dealers received and gave checks on a similar basis. The same shares being transacted over and over again, sometimes daily, would give rise to a very large number of post-dated checks, each one bigger than the other, and which theoretically would be honored, each one backing the other. If one was paid another could be paid, etc. On the other hand if one defaulted they would all default, which is naturally what happened.

In early 1982, the region started to have substantial worries. The war between Iran and Iraq which had started in Iraq's favor, turned more towards Iran. Further the slide of OPEC's market share and the lower petroleum prices made the local investors a bit wary of the overall stability of the Gulf. Some Kuwaitis felt they should perhaps withdraw from the Souk Al Manakh and hence in August 1982 some of the post-dated checks which had come due bounced. Thus the whole system collapsed.

The Kuwaiti parliament took issue with the government, and demanded that the Central Bank start unravelling the situation. The total amount of checks outstanding stood at US$ 94 billion, of which 95 per cent were drawn by only 17 traders.[12] Immediately the government set up a company, Kuwait Clearing Company (KUCLEAR), to sort out the checks, write down the premium charged and collect the lowered face values of the checks so that each investor could pay the other. Unfortunately the numbers and amounts of the transactions were such that four years later the problem is not yet completely unravelled.

The government also stepped in to protect the small investors. They defined the small investors as the persons who had less than KD 2 million (US$ 7 million) in the market; in view of the liquidity problems in Kuwait, this amount was later cut to KD 500,000.[13] The 'small investors' were able to recover payment from the government by receiving part in cash and part in government dinar bonds; the smaller the investor the larger the cash payment.

The first steps taken by the government to resolve the stock market crisis were of course helpful. However confidence was not restored to the market. The problems were very much compounded by a sudden and related crisis in real estate. As was explained earlier, the government had systematically injected money into the country by buying

and selling lands to the citizens. As a result there was great speculation in land values, knowing that in the end the government would
buy the land at a profit to the seller. In fact some of the companies
created to be traded on the stock exchange were real estate companies,
the goals of which were to deal in land in Kuwait and in the Emirates.
With the decline in revenues, the government was no longer able to
buy lands at a premium, which in turn decreased the revenues of the
citizens, which in turn stopped them from buying from one another,
thereby cancelling the real estate market altogether. The government
decreased its land purchases from 22.4 per cent of current spending
in 1980/1 to 5.0 per cent in 1984/5.[14]

A large part of the activities of the investors both in shares and
real estate had been financed by the banks. The local Kuwaiti banks
as well as the banks in Bahrain, and some large Western banks lent
large amounts of money secured by what they thought were perfectly
safe assets. Some of these loans were even syndicated in the Eurodollar
market with great publicity. Some banks became specialized in this
field. Indeed one can trace the collapse of the Arab Asian Bank in
Bahrain to this type of facility. The loans were secured by mortgages
on land in Kuwait, and by pledges on Gulf shares. Once both the real
estate and the share market collapsed the banks had no security left;
the investors having lost all were not able to repay the banks; and
very large loans eventually had to be placed by the banks on their
list of criticized facilities.

The total amount of bad loans in Kuwait has been estimated by
MEES, *MEED*, and the *Financial Times* to be between KD 1.7 and
2.2 billion (US$ 6 to 7.7 billion), while the aggregate capital and
reserves of the banks are not more than KD 1.2 billion (US$ 4.2
billion). Naturally the government of Kuwait is aware of the difficult
situation which exists and has pledged to support the banks and help
them work out their difficult loans.

In spite of the government reassurance the public has remained
wary of the overall situation. The bank shares have remained very
low, and again this has added to the problems of the banks because
of the very large loans advanced by the banks to their own directors
and secured by the shares in the banks themselves (KD 276 million,
see p. 27 above). Whenever the value of the bank shares decreases,
the value of the security held by the banks also decreases, the quality
of the portfolio declines which in turn affects the market price of the
shares, thereby creating a downward spiral. The government realizes
the importance of keeping the banks afloat, as they are the heart of
the Kuwaiti economy, and is absolutely committed to saving the

banks and hence re-establishing trust in the basic financial system in the country. On 13 October 1985 Jassem al Khorafi, the then Minister of Finance, stated that the government had placed with the commercial and specialized banks deposits totaling KD 2,965 million (US$ 9,960 million).[15] These deposits were not necessarily placed in the safest banks, hence emphasizing that the purpose was to support the banks and the financial system in Kuwait. For example the Bank of Bahrain and Kuwait with a capital of only KD 13.9 million received KD 398 million of deposits — 28 times its capital; while the National Bank of Kuwait with a capital of KD 189 million received KD 452 million — 6.6 times its capital.

The task however was, and still is, formidable and costly. It has been estimated that the government had spent more than US$ 7 billion by August 1983 just to support the markets and pay the small investors.[16] The investment companies controlled by the government channelled funds to some of the largest debtors who then were able to repay part of their debts. KIC and KFTCIC lent a total of KD 597 million to 17 individuals. These loans are secured by assets estimated in late 1985 to KD 257 million. However, with the continuous fall in the stock and the real estate market the securities are probably worth substantially less than mentioned. Among the 17 major borrowers is Sheikh Khalifah Abdallah Al Khalifah who owes KFTCIC a record KD 278 million (US$ 1,011 million) secured by properties worth KD 38 million.[17]

The clearing company set up by the government, KUCLEAR, and the fund for small investors were successful enough that by the early part of 1986 enough progress had been made to see the focus of government effort move from the US$ 90 billion clearing problem to the no less difficult problem of ensuring the viability of the banking system.

The official stock exchange which had opened in April 1977 also suffered from the crash. The exchange had been created to stop the unchecked dealings and speculation which had led to the various crises mentioned earlier. At the end of 1977, 40 companies were listed on the exchange covering 95 million shares and a total capital of 10 million dinars. There were 22 purely private companies and 18 from the joint sector. The crash of the Souk Al Manakh made most investors very short of cash and naturally forced them to start selling their portfolio of purely Kuwaiti shares, which in turn brought a decline in the prices on the official market in line with the decrease in the Souk Al Manakh.

Eventually the government intervened to maintain the prices and again KFTCIC and other government-controlled agencies started buying shares. On 18 May 1985 the finance minister said that the government had lost KD 455.1 million (US$ 1.51 billion) in reserves to support the official stock exchange. The loss was computed by taking the amounts actually spent to support the market, about US$ 2.52 billion and the market value of the shares that day.[18] In fact the potential loss could be higher since the prices of shares have since declined. The government is faced with keeping the shares until better days but at the additional costs of: (1) virtually nationalizing the companies in which it is now a major shareholder; and (2) losing the revenues it should have earned from these monies if they had been placed abroad.

Losses will not be only borne by the government, but also by all who are holding shares. *MEES* in January 1986 quoted Al-Shal Bureau, a prominent financial consultant in Kuwait, as assessing the decline in the share values since 1983 at 74 per cent, or a decrease in the real aggregate book value of all the companies listed of US$ 24 billion.

At 31 March 1985 the Kuwaiti government had directly or indirectly majority ownership of 3 banks (out of 8), 2 insurance companies (out of 4), 2 investment companies (out of 3 public companies) and 3 real estate companies (out of 6).[19] In fact since some of the companies in which the government has become a major shareholder are very large, it now appears (according to the *Financial Times* special supplement of 25 February 1986, p. 12) that the government owns more than 50 per cent of the official market shares.

The ministry of finance has tried to re-instill some trust into the market by creating a new stock exchange (in late 1984). The new exchange works under a new set of rules:

— The management of the new Kuwait stock exchange will be supervised by a committee which will include the minister of finance, representatives of the Chamber of Commerce, the Central Bank and stock brokers.

— Bids must be made in writing.

— Groups of shares are to be divided in 'units' of 500 to 100,000 shares depending on the face value of the share and no order can be for more than 25 units (the purpose of this regulation is to avoid wide price fluctuations in the market).

— The authorities of the stock exchange have the right to examine the financial situation of the companies listed, and will publish full financial details on same.

— The main stock exchange will list 39 public shareholding companies and 7 closed companies. An official parallel market will be created on the main floor which will list 30 Gulf companies, but which will be traded only for 1½ hours daily.

— The companies listed on the exchange will pay an annual fee of KD 10,000 plus 0.001 per cent of their capital.

— Stockbroking firms owned by individuals are not allowed and stockbroking companies must have a minimum capital of KD 100,000 and provide a deposit of KD 250,000 as security against malpractice.

— Only 11 stockbroking firms have been licensed, and their employees must attend training sessions of 16 weeks on trading and financial knowledge.

— Only two companies are allowed to act as market makers, i.e. allowed to quote bid and sell prices and be forced to take shares offered at the quoted prices.

— Kuwaiti dinar bonds will eventually be listed on the exchange.[20]

The regulations, no doubt, will clean-up the market and bring it near to the standards of more financially developed nations. However it has not had an immediate effect on share values. In 1985 alone the aggregate share values dropped 44.82 per cent for Kuwaiti companies and 45.66 per cent for Gulf shares, corresponding to a value of KD 2.1 billion (US$ 7.8 billion).[21]

To emphasize the clean-up campaign the Central Bank of Kuwait reviewed the financial standing of 79 money changing establishments and 38 investment companies. In October 1985 the government temporarily suspended trading of all Gulf shares until a full assessment of their values was made. The Central Bank reviewed the 33 Gulf companies listed on the new official 'parallel' stock market and advised that of these 4 should be liquidated, 4 merged, 11 should change their boards of directors, and 10 change their executive managements. The Central Bank also reviewed 62 closed companies and reported that only 6 were profitable, 3 had closed, 25 should be liquidated, 5 should merge and 3 were in acceptable shape.[22]

The debate still continues on how to deal with the Gulf companies. One proposal put forward by the government is that it should buy the shares of the Gulf companies so as to repatriate money into Kuwait. The cash paid would help the banks repay some of their bad debts. Once taken over, the government could strip the companies of their assets or liquidate them to raise the cash to pay itself back. The first proposed cash outlay would be expected to be KD 400 million, but the government estimated that its net cost would amount to less than

KD 12.2 million, which indeed would be a bargain.[23]

In April 1986, the government did announce that KIA, the 'holding company' for the country's investments, would start purchasing the shares of the closed companies still in existence, and which have cooperated with the ministry of finance.[24] As of 22 April 1986 the government had bought 367.7 million shares for a total of US$ 410 million, paid half in cash and half in three-year non-interest bearing government bonds.[25] In early May 1986, KIA had finalized its purchase of 33 closed Kuwaiti and Gulf companies at a cost of KD 140.4 million (US$ 475 million). KIA will liquidate 23 of these companies.[26] The cost of the May 1986 purchase is below the original estimate, but the net cost after liquidation may be much higher than the KD 12.2 million mentioned to the National Assembly in December 1985, as most of the assets of the companies being liquidated are unsellable. On the other hand the cash paid by KIA will help the bank reduce the bad debts of the banks and comfort the economic system.

The same argument has been used to push for a merger of all the Bahrain-based banks created with a large base of Kuwaiti money to capitalize on the Souk Al Manakh. These banks (Bahrain International Bank, United Gulf Bank, Bahrain Middle East Bank, etc.) have a total capital of over US$ 1 billion. If merged and partially liquidated, down to say US$ 200 million, one should expect that US$ 800 million should in principle return to Kuwait. These banks had their capital paid in when formed, and have not had time to develop a great deal since then. Their total assets do not add up to more than US$ 4 billion. If merged and reduced to a joint capital of US$ 200 million, the new bank could still carry the same assets. However some of these banks could have a combined total of bad loans of US$ 200 million, which, if written off, would decrease the capital to nothing. To preserve the new merged bank as a real live entity, the merged bank could only be liquidated down to US$ 400-500 million capital, which would reduce the funds which could be repatriated to Kuwait. The mergers would create a great deal of friction between the various shareholders, boards of directors and top managements; for example, what criterion would the Kuwaiti government use to decide which board members and which managements to eliminate? And undoubtedly the shareholders of each of the banks would feel slighted if they had to take a loss on their investment because of bad loans which have been made by another bank. Further, the Bahraini authorities may not be pleased to see the elimination of a number of banks at the cost of jobs in Bahrain. It could be that the unknown problems which a merger of the banks could create may not render that merger attractive to the various parties concerned.

The problems created by the crash of the market in Kuwait are such that one can hope it will not happen again. On the other hand one can feel that the events of 1982 were almost fated. The regulations which the government issued in 1977 were devised to avoid the exact problems which took place later. Unfortunately, the regulations, once issued, were not enforced. In fact the regulations themselves, as mentioned, made the speculators develop their activities in the unofficial parallel market over which the government had no control. Of course, many in the government and in the royal family were greatly active in the parallel market, which may have decreased substantially the government's will to control the development of the Souk Al Manakh, and of the use of post-dated checks.

Overall it appears that the problem of the Souk Al Manakh was probably due to the newness of the markets in the region as a whole when faced with an immense increase in personal income. Whatever regulations or controls were imposed by the government they would most likely have been circumvented by the extremely clever and imaginative Kuwaiti financiers. By the same token, in this present period of very low cash flow in the region, the incentives for developing new instruments and market techniques are just not there, and hence one can expect the stock market in Kuwait to become more mature and staid.

The crash of the market will certainly not be forgotten by the Kuwaitis and the other Gulf Arabs for some time. In the long run, however, it will appear in the history books as a small chapter similar to those discussing the South Sea bubble in London, the tulip bulb scandal in Holland or the *assignats* scandal in France.

In Saudi Arabia the perception by the minister of finance that the government must exert constant control over the economy has been successful in stopping the development of a healthy stock market. In Kuwait the lack of enforcement of government controls, and for all intents and purposes the involvement of some of the government members and relatives in the free capitalistic market, has achieved an almost similar result — that all major corporations have become controlled directly or indirectly by the government, and the population is subject to the goodwill of the government's handouts.

NOTES

1. Industrial Studies and Development Center, *Guide to industrial investment in Saudi Arabia*, 4th edn, Riyadh, 1975, p. 21.

2. Abdul Rahman Ibrahim Eshaq, 'Gulf stockmarkets: change of attitude is necessary', in *Arab banking and finance handbook*, Falcon, Bahrain, 1985, p. 117.

3. Ibid., p. 117.

4. Industrial Studies and Development Center, *Guide to industrial investment in Saudi Arabia*, p. 68; SAMA, *Annual report*, Riyadh,1404, p. 166.

5. *Financial Times*, 'Survey of Saudi Arabia', 26 April 1982, p. 11.

6. Abdul Rahman and Ibrahim Eshaq, 'Gulf stockmarkets'.

7. *Arab Banking and Finance*, July 1982, p. 33.

8. The index used to compute the fall of 70 per cent since December 1983 is provided by the National Bank of Kuwait Economic and Financial Bulletin, November 1985, p. 23.

9. Mehran Nakhjavani, 'Plus ça change . . .', article in *Arab banking and finance handbook*, Falcon, Bahrain, 1983, pp. 109-11.

10. Yunis Asa'ad, *The legal and practical guide to doing business in Kuwait*, Kuwait, 1979, vol. 3, p. 12.

11. Mehran Nakhjavani, 'Plus ça change . . .'.

12. *Financial Times*, 12 October 1983, p. 27.

13. *Middle East Economic Survey*, vol. 28, no. 28, p. B1.

14. Ibid., vol. 29, no. 5, p. B1.

15. Ibid., vol. 29, no. 2, p. B2.

16. *Arab Banking and Finance*, August 1983, p. 43.

17. *Middle East Economic Survey*, vol. 29, no. 13, p. B2.

18. *Middle East Economic Survey*, vol. 28, no. 33, p. B1.

19. Ibid., p. B3.

20. Abdul Muttalib Al Sairafi, 'A new era in Kuwait stock market', article in *Arab banking and finance handbook*, Falcon, Bahrain, 1985, pp. 141-6.

21. *Middle East Economic Survey*, vol. 29, no. 14, p. B5.

22. *Middle East Economic Digest*, 7 December 1985, p. 22.

23. Ibid.

24. *Middle East Economic Survey*, vol. 29, no. 26, p. B2.

25. *Middle East Economic Digest*, 3 May 1986.

26. *Middle East Economic Survey*, vol. 29, no. 31, p. B3.

5

The Islamic Banks

Whatever you give (in grant or as a present) to require an increase to the monies of donors will not drive credit with God; whatever alms (Zakat) you give for God's sake, you get double in return.

Holy Qur'an, Surat ar Rum, v. 39

Oh ye who have believed do not eat usury which is multiples and fear God hoping to win enjoyment and peace in eternal life after death.

Holy Qur'an, Surat Al Imran, v. 130

Those who eat usury will only rise (from their graves) just like the rise of a person who has been inflicted with mental instability by the devil and that is because they (who eat usury) said that trading is like Usury and God has allowed trading and banned Usury; he who receives a sermon from his God and deceases (from eating Usury) shall have what he had already taken (prior to the ban) and his absolution rests with God, and those who recommit Usury are residents of hell where they are eternal. God shall strip Usury of all the blessings and increase the alms and double the merit; God does not like sinful renegades (who make usury legitimate). Those who believed, have performed benevolences, performed prayers and paid Zakat will be rewarded by God and there is no fear for them nor shall they be grieved. Oh ye believers. If you fail to do so be advised that God and His Messenger will wage war on you; if you repent you may recover your capital without taking an increase or recovering less than the capital sum; he who is in financial straits, let him wait for better times and if you give alms (discharge the liability of an insolvent) it would be better for you, if you know it is good.

Holy Qur'an, Surat al Baqara, vv. 275-80

Sami Hassan al Homood, in a doctoral dissertation at the University of Cairo, quoted the above verses in the Holy Qur'an as being the basic tenets by which God revealed to Mohammed the interdiction of charging and taking of interest on money, or for that matter any other commodity lent by one person to another.

In this chapter the writer will not discuss the theological aspect of the ban on usury or on whether the word 'riba' really means usury, nor whether the charging of interest by banks and other financial institutions can or cannot be considered usury. We will assume, as appears to be the case in most literature on this matter, that the Holy Qur'an expresses the interdiction by God of any form of interest. We will however review the institutions created in the past few years to bring life to this concept, especially those presently based in the Arabian Gulf. We will also evaluate if in actual practice the type of services which the Islamic financial institutions are providing are conforming to the original concept of interest-free lending and borrowing.

For the sake of fairness, it must be pointed out that the interdiction of interest is by no means the reserved domain of Islam. It is well known that medieval Europe, under the then all-encompassing domination of Christianity, was adverse to the concept of interest and usually let the Jews act as the bankers to the kings and nobles. The first Christian bankers appeared in Italy, and spread throughout Europe in the early days of the Renaissance. The Christian feelings about interest came from verses in the Old Testament:

> You shall not charge interest on anything you lend to a fellow countryman, money or food or anything else on which interest can be charged.
> You may charge interest on a loan to a foreigner but not on a loan to a fellow-countryman, for then the Lord your God will bless you in all you undertake in the land which you are entering to occupy.
>
> Deuteronomy, 23, 19

> Consider the man who is righteous and does what is just and right . . . He gives bread to the hungry and clothes to those who have none. He never lends at discount or at interest. He shuns injustice and deals fairly between a man and man.
>
> Ezekiel, 18, 8

The quotations from the Bible are mentioned by Al Homood in his dissertation, although presented in another translation (the above are quoted from the New English Bible published by Cambridge and Oxford University Presses). They are from the Old Testament and hence apply to the Jews as well as to the Christians and the Moslems. Therefore, it seems to the writer that none of the 'religions of the book' (Christian, Jew or Moslem) can claim more righteousness than the other, nor for that matter more of a true understanding of God's orders by its followers.

Much has been written and suggested on the real meaning of usury, interest, etc. For example, it has been suggested that inflation rates should be netted out of real interest rates to compute how much usury, if any, is being really charged; and it has been suggested that interest is only the cost of using capital, just like profit is the cost of using and purchasing any commodities.

In all religious matters, as perhaps in all secular matters, the Truth is only the interpretation by very imperfect mortals of Divine wishes. No one can or should take the cloak of God to express opinions and interpretations on what the wish of God is. We can only compare the internal logic of the human arguments. In no way can a disagreement on the part of this writer (or of any other persons) on what is being done in the name of Islam or Christianity or Judaism reflect on the essence and undoubted value of each of the religions.

In the present revival and fervor of modern Islam, the words Islamic banking have created great expectations and realizations. There are presently 62 Islamic institutions in the world, created by private Moslem citizens. There are also all the Islamic banks and institutions of Pakistan and Iran where the existing banks were forced by the governments to become Islamic and adhere to the principle of no interest.

The Nasser Social Bank founded in 1972 in Egypt is the grandfather of Islamic banks. This institution remained the only Islamic bank until 1977 when the first brainchildren of Prince Mohammed Al Faysal bin Abdelaziz Al Saud were started: the Faisal Islamic bank of Egypt and the Faisal Islamic Bank of Sudan. These two banks were followed eventually by the creation of the world headquarters of the Faisal banks, the Dar Al Mal Al Islami, in Geneva. Dar Al Mal had a declared capital of US\$ 1,000 million, with US\$ 310 million paid in. The same year the Kuwait Finance House was founded in Kuwait with a capital of KD 15 million (US\$ 52 million).

In 1982 Sheikh Saleh Kamel, a prominent, albeit low profile, Saudi businessman started Al Baraka Investment and Development Company in Jeddah, with a reported paid in capital of US\$ 500 million. Al Baraka became the holding company for ten other Islamic institutions in the world. With the large capital available to the companies of Al Baraka group, the banks may not have been as dependent on private and small depositors as other Islamic banks and hence did not feel they had to bandy about the name of Islam. Sheikh Saleh has been quoted as saying:

Islamic banking and finance provokes an immediate reaction. I don't like referring to it in those terms. There are too many institutions called Islamic this and Islamic that. I think it's wrong to invoke the name of Islam in business. What I wanted was an institution that could develop both merchant and investment financial services without recourse to usury.[1]

The main investment company of the Al Baraka group is based in Bahrain. It is called the Al Baraka Investment Company and is headed by no other than Sami Hassan Al Homood, from whose doctoral dissertation we have quoted earlier, and will quote much more later.

The Islamic financial institutions which were first started in the Middle East quickly tried to develop activities outside the Moslem world. Dar Al Mal tried to obtain a license to open in London and thus gain a certain degree of respectability among the Western financial markets. However the application was turned down by the Central Bank of England. The Governor of the Central Bank was quoted by *Arab Banking and Finance* in November 1984 as saying: 'although Islamic banking tenets provided a perfectly acceptable mode of investment, they did not fall within long-established, well understood definitions of what constitutes banking in the UK'. The article went on, saying that 'the point he made was that Western banking regulations insisted on capital based security for depositors. Moreover, deposits were not regarded as liabilities on an Islamic bank's balance sheet. The depositor had to take part in all the risks and profits and losses of the institution.'

The Governor of the Central Bank of England did not mention the questions which had been raised in the financial community about the management and goals of the Dar Al Mal group. Indeed in 1982/3 the Geneva bank had lost US$ 279 million on bullion trading.[2] It was also well known in 1984 that the group had substantial numbers of difficult loans to Sudan, a country with only limited ability to repay its debts, and to a Saudi company owned by a cousin of HRH Prince Mohammed, in which the Prince was a major shareholder, and which was eventually placed into liquidation in Riyadh. It was assumed by most bankers that the creditors had only a very remote chance of being repaid. One could speculate that perhaps the objections of the Bank of England had more to do with the personalities involved in Dar Al Mal than with the actual concept of interest free banking.

In fact Sheikh Saleh Kamel, a much less controversial figure, was able to obtain permission from the Bank of England to buy a licensed deposit-taking bank called Hargrave Securities, which conducts full commercial banking activities. It also allowed Al Baraka to establish a full Islamic operation, although under the title of investment company, rather than bank with deposit-taking privileges.

Nevertheless, Sir Leigh Pemberton touched one of the major points at the heart of Islamic banking today. Western banking insists on having the liabilities of a bank come before the capital of the shareholders in the case of liquidation. In other words, the deposits in a bank, which are the bank's liabilities, are the responsibility of the shareholders to the extent of their capital. It is very common in bank bankruptcies in the United States to see that the depositors are guaranteed their money while the shareholders funds are cancelled totally and the shares literally given to another institution which then assumes the management and the safety of the deposits to the extent of its capital. This action takes place hundreds of times each year under the control of either the Federal Deposit Insurance Corporation (FDIC) which insures federally chartered banks, the Federal Savings and Loans Insurance Corporation (FSLIC) which supervises the takeover of savings and loans banks, or the state controllers for locally chartered banks. In the case of the Savings and Loans banks, which at the time of high interest rates in the late 1970s up to the mid-1980s went through very difficult times, the Federal Savings and Loans Insurance Company (FSLIC) and the relevant state authorities arranged for larger institutions to take over failed institutions, became responsible for all the deposits, netted out all the bad loans against the existing capital and asked the new institutional owner only to add some fresh capital in the failed bank.

Perhaps one should propose a similar type of controlling agency on all the Islamic banks in the world so as to ensure the security of the depositors'/co-investors' investments at the expense of the founding members or of management, if both founders and management fail to protect the unsuspecting depositors from unprofessional behavior.

The basic concept of modern Islamic banking is that since interest is forbidden but profits allowed, one should develop investments in which one can be a full partner and therefore obtain a share of the profits from the transaction. To make matters easy to handle, the partners pool their funds in a partnership which in turn invests the pool in various endeavours. The partners are also therefore the depositors. In most Islamic institutions the depositors have the right to leave their funds in the pool for the length of time they desire (as in a normal bank); but, naturally, they can expect to receive a greater share of the profits the longer they leave their funds. The depositors in the normal course of business will come in or go out of the pool of funds. It is hoped that enough deposits will on the average remain sufficient to continue funding whatever project has been financed. The original capital of the founding members can make up the shortfalls in deposits, if any. Since the depositors are partners they cannot have any assurance that their investment will be profitable or for that matter safe. Indeed, it could even be lost.

Al Homood discussed the debates that took place on the matter of the liability of what he calls the common active partner, which in this case is the Islamic bank, and hence its owners and management, but concluded that 'it is not sound to urge the assumption of liability for that which has not initially been guaranteed to be returned'.[3]

The great problem, in the writer's opinion, is that the depositor and hence partner becomes prisoner of the management of the Islamic bank, without the cushion which was given to him by the capital of the regular banking institutions. Of course, a similar risk exists in any mutual fund in the Western world. However the financial markets in the West have had plenty of time to establish who was professional and who was not. Further, and most important, the type of investments made by the mutual funds, and the results and the management are subject to extensive disclosure requirements which at any rate help the investor make an educated assessment of the type of risk he is willing to take, and thus, the type of return he may expect. It appears that a bad name has been given to Islamic banking by operators which used the system of partnership to part well-meaning Moslems from their savings. To date it does not appear that the depositors in the Islamic banks and investment companies have any say in the management of the funds nor in the type of risks which should be taken; nor are they represented or protected by proper regulatory institutions.

Al Homood compares the rules to be imposed on the management of Islamic partnerships to a car or bus passenger's requests to the driver:

> . . . in the former case [the chauffeured car], the hirer of the vehicle may require the driver to proceed to any place to which he wishes to go and may also ask him to change direction at his discretion; but on the other hand, a person using the public transport may not, not to say imagine, require the driver to change course of the route which is set for him from beginning to end.

He continues:

> Therefore it is inevitable that a common active partner should be empowered to determine the conditions which conform to the nature of the common collective investment; this means that a common

active partner enjoys full independence . . .[4]

However, it seems to the writer that one cannot blindly trust that one's funds are safe just because they are invested in an 'Islamic institution'. The term by itself does not guarantee that the managers of the funds are really good and honest Moslems, nor does it guarantee that they are competent.

A good example of the risks of Islamic investments as it has been sometimes structured is given by a group known as Arbab Al Maal (AAM). The activities of this group were reported by *Arab Banking and Finance* in January 1985. The article went a long way in explaining the investment scheme. Tanzania has potential gold mines which need capital to be exploited. Tanzania also owes US$ 10 million to a surveying company which delimited the location and wealth of the gold mines, and which is owned by an East German national called Mr Gollmer. The company, Geosurvey, is well known and reputable but has had great difficulties in getting paid by some of the African countries where it has worked. In order to get paid by Tanzania Gollmer has given a certain Ibrahim Kamel (no relations to Saleh Kamel of Al Baraka) an option to buy 51 per cent of his company.

To arrange the repayment to Geosurvey and the exploitation of the mines Kamel formed an Islamic investment company called Arbab Al-Maal based on the principle of mudaraba. AAM is capitalized at US$ 25 million which is provided by the public in general, mostly from the Arabian Gulf. AAM gives full control of its operation to a manager (Kamel). The US$ 25 million is then divided as follows:

— A loan of US$ 10 million is made by AAM to the government of Tanzania, who will use the money to repay the debt to the surveying company, and who in essence will grant the right to mine.
— US$ 10 million will go to a corporation called Dar Tadine Al-Umma (UDT) who will itself fund and manage the actual mining through a local corporation called Dar Tadine Tanzania.
— US$5 million will go to Kamel as commission to put the deal together.

The gold to be mined by UDT will be split one-sixth to Kamel, one-third to Tanzania, and the balance to UDT. The government of Tanzania will then repay its debt to AAM through its share in the gold. The article in *Arab Banking and Finance* estimated that the mines hold 500,000 tons of gold ore, expected to yield 3 to 4 grams of gold per ton. If such is the case, the total output of the mine will be 2 tons of gold, or 67,000 ounces at US$ 350 per ounce representing about US$ 23.5 million.

If the total return is estimated properly it shows that Tanzania will get approximately US$ 8 million. UDT will get US$12 million and Kamel US$ 4 million added to the US$ 5 million he is scheduled to obtain up front. In the final analysis AAB puts in US$ 25 million and gets US$ 8 million reimbursement from Tanzania and US$ 12 million from the gold, minus the costs of actually mining and refining the ore, which undoubtedly are substantial. At any rate AAB will lose not less than US$ 5 million and probably most of its investment, while Kamel gets cash US$ 9 million, plus 51 per cent of Geosurvey's 'new, improved' net worth. Tanzania for its share will get nothing except a decrease in its liability to Geosurvey.

AAB organized as a mudaraba provides an Islamic contract of co-operation. The mudaraba gives day-to-day responsibility to a mudarib (Kamel) who has full control of the operation. The shares of profit are defined as it should be and the fees are mentioned up front. Nevertheless, in spite of the formal adherence to the Islamic principles which have been defined by such authorities as Al Homood, one cannot but equate the project to a clever scheme, playing on men's greed for gold, whether they be Moslems or animists.

The instrument used in the investment above is the mudaraba, where the capital is provided to a promoter who is responsible for the management. Profits, if any, are distributed according to pre-agreed formula. However, the risk is borne by the provider of capital.

There other forms of instruments which have been developed by the Islamic institutions and which are in use in Iran and Pakistan as well as in the Islamic banks and companies throughout the world. Dr Ziauddin Ahmad, the Director General of the International Institute of Islamic Economics at Islamabad, Pakistan, described the instruments in the following terms:[5]

— Musharaka: A cooperative agreement under which the Islamic bank provides funds which mingle with the funds of the business enterprise and others. All providers of capital are entitled to participate in management but not necessarily required to do so. Profit is distributed among the partners in preagreed ratios while loss is borne by each partner strictly in proportion to respective capital contribution . . .

— Murabaha: A contract in which a client wishing to purchase equipment or goods requests the Islamic bank to purchase the items and sell them to him at cost plus a declared profit.

— Bai-Muajjal: A trade deal in which the seller allows the buyer to pay the price of a commodity at a future date in lump sum or installments. The price fixed for the commodity in such transaction can be the same as the spot price or higher or lower than the spot price.

— Bai-Salam: A trade deal in which the buyer pays the agreed price of a commodity in advance and the commodity is delivered to the buyer at a specified future date.

— Ijara: An arrangement under which the Islamic bank leases an equipment, building or other facility for the client against an agreed rental, together with an undertaking from the client to make additional payments in an account which will eventually permit the client to purchase the equipment, building or facility.

— Qard or Qard Hasanah: Qard is a loan transaction in which the client undertakes to repay the principal at a stipulated future time but on which no interest is charged . . . [it] is a more benevolent type of loan without any service charge or repayment schedule . . .

Not all these products are accepted by Islamic banks as being Islamic. Al Homood, in *Islamic Banking*, discusses forward deals at length and, citing the Hadith, concludes that there is usury if there is delivery of goods but no immediate payment. He also says: 'Usury is inherent in any forward exchange.'[6] This statement appears to negate the Bai-Muajjal and Bai-Salam.

These financial products of course must compete against the products developed over the years by the established banks. When faced with competition, the Islamic banks must contend with some flaws which appear to exist in these products. The flaws which we will discuss presently do not reflect the impossibility of Islamic banking, but only the difficulty of finding the proper and new instruments in a very crowded and competitive field.

In the Arabian Gulf banking is very competitive, and most of the products available in the Western banking world are available to all citizens, hence they can easily compare the benefits of both Islamic and non-Islamic type products. It does appear that, in the Gulf, the Islamic institutions have not fared very well. Out of the 61 existing institutions worldwide, there are four in Bahrain, one in Kuwait, and five in Saudi, the cradle of Islam. Further, in Saudi Arabia one of the banks is owned by the Moslem government and is really a multinational organization active outside the kingdom, two are holding companies of other banks and not active in the country either, and only two may obtain permission to work in the kingdom, although their licenses are still pending.

Some of the citizens of the Gulf have complained that the Islamic banks are more expensive than the regular banks. In some cases this is a fair evaluation. Let us take an example cited by Al Homood where he considers the purchase of a taxi cab through an Ijara agreement. The purchase cost is 2,400 Jordanian dinars. Net income after salary and expenses is JD 60 per month. The Islamic bank offers to finance the cab on the basis of 25 per cent of net income, i.e. JD 180 per year. The balance, JD 540 per annum, is placed in a repayment account. When the repayment account has been credited by JD 2,400, i.e. after 4½ years the bank transfers the title deed to the driver. According to Al Homood the potential borrower 'did not believe what he heard and in no time expressed his approval'.

Of course, one can look at the same transaction from another angle. If the same cab driver had borrowed from a regular bank the full value of the cab at say 12 per cent per annum for 4½ years, his payments would have been JD 693 per annum. He would have owned the cab from day 1. His total interest payments to the bank over the life of the loan would have been JD 718. Under the Islamic contract above the driver would have paid to the lender JD 810 in 'profit sharing'. In all fairness, interest may be higher than 12 per cent, but then again the profit sharing arrangement could be higher than 25 per cent.

Another example given by Al Homood uses a Musharaka contract:

A cloth trader from Amman imported 100,000 meters of popular cloth from East Germany; according to his book records, the computation of the cost of the transaction was as follows. The price . . . (including freight, insurance, import license, expenses of bank which opened the credit for JD 90, and custom duties) total JD 9,390.

The entire quantity of the cloth was sold within three months of the date of arrival; the meter of cloth was sold for 110 fils; the profit realized from this transaction was JD 11,000 − JD 9,390 = JD 1,610.

The period from the commencement of the agreement to purchase until the sale of the entire consignment was eight months.

We talked to the trader concerned and discussed with him

whether he was prepared to accept joint financing of the transaction by the non-usury bank . . . where the bank would pay the value of the documents on receipt, plus the customs duty and the costs of clearing the goods until they reached the trader's warehouses, where the trader would take 75% of the profit and the bank 25%, on condition that if the goods perish or suffer a loss, it shall be shared commensurately with the participation of each party.[7]

This transaction would bring the Islamic bank a gross profit of JD 402 plus JD 90 for the letter of credit fees, and JD 30 for foreign exchange commissions, i.e. a total of JD 522. A similar transaction could naturally be financed by the trader at his usual commercial bank. His cost would then be:

L/c fee	90
Cost of foreign exchange ½%	30
Interest 90 days at 12% p.a.	282
Total	JD 402

It appears that in this case the trader would be loath to use the Islamic bank. His only advantage is that should he be unable to sell his cloth, or to sell at a loss, the Islamic bank would also absorb some of the loss. On the other hand, the bank, to protect itself, will naturally try to deal only with the very best traders who will provide a high degree of confidence ensuring that the bank will be able to recoup its funds. In fact the good and profitable trader will mostly likely prefer to deal with his regular bank, which will take less of his profits, than the Islamic institution.

We could take numbers of other examples and eventually come to the conclusion that the costs of Islamic banking products are very close to those of regular banks.

In Jordan where these examples were taken, the banking sector was, at the time, somewhat antiquated, and indeed the costs charged by the regular commercial banks may have been higher than the 12 per cent mentioned here. In countries where banking is more modern and competitive, the prices reviewed are close to reality, and indeed in the writer's opinion partly explains why the Islamic banks have not been successful in the Gulf. Islamic banks have developed the most in countries of dire poverty. The hopes and aspirations of people subject to difficult economic conditions, and usually a general mismanagement of their economies such as in Egypt or Sudan make them feel that Islamic banks are a Godsend. However in countries like Bahrain where all systems are allowed and the country is running well, the Islamic banks have not made a mark in the markets.

There appears also to be some misconception on the part of even the best Islamic bank officials on what 'risk' is. Ziauddin Ahmad, Director General of the International Institute of Islamic Economics at the University of Islamabad, Pakistan, said:

> The interest system is disallowed in Islam because intrinsically it is a highly inequitable system. The feature that makes the interest system inequitable is that the provider of capital funds is assured of a fixed return while all the risk is borne by the user of these capital funds. Justice, which is the hallmark of the Islamic system demands that the provider of capital funds should share the risk with the entrepreneur if he wishes to earn a profit.[8]

Al Homood echoes and reinforces the same thought when he says that:

> where money is given to the user as a loan, the credits are given to wealthy people who can provide a collateral guarantee. Those who are not wealthy can only sell their efforts, i.e. be workers. In such a society an honest engineer, a qualified physician or an experienced farmer are not allowed to have the finance for beginning an independent life by establishing a factory, a hospital or a farm.[9]

Such views seem to say that banks do not take risks and hence are not entitled to interest. This approach seems to have been influenced more by a somewhat simplistic Marxist approach, than by the Holy Qur'an. However, this thinking seems to dominate most of the literature on Islamic banking. It seems that, in reality, the ability to be loaned to is not dominated either by wealth, or by the ability to give collateral. A lender, whether Islamic or otherwise, will or should make his loans a function of the evaluation of risk. If a loan is made to a poorly managed venture, or to persons of poor repute, chances are that the money will be lost, whether there is interest or profit sharing involved.

In traditional banking the evaluation of risk always is, or at any rate should be, done on the basis that if an endeavor turns sour, the bank as well as the promoter of the endeavor will lose money. The banks which lent to the Soviet Union prior to 1917, or those which lent to the thousands of firms that went bankrupt during the great depression in the United States, or even today those which have lent to any firm that went into chapter eleven (the American bankruptcy law) can vouch for this effect.

In general, large corporate loans are unsecured, and if indeed the banks obtain an interest income at a given percentage rate every year, they are also in a position to lose their funds. Secured lending is of course available, especially to borrowers without a history of good credit, who otherwise could not borrow at all. The decision on lending is made not on the fact that 'the honest engineer . . . is allowed to have finance for beginning an independent life', but mainly on the evaluation of the honest engineer's ability to manage his future business and the soundness of his concept. In fact one can wonder how a loan could be extended by any bank, even if Islamic, to any individual or firm if it was unable to feel confident that the money would be returned after it had filled the need of the borrower.

Part of the training of any banker is to learn that collateral is only an added safety to a loan decision. If a loan can only be granted if it is properly secured by real estate, gold or whatever, it should not be made. The textbooks are filled with examples of loans made against diamonds, precious metals, paintings, even real estate, which eventually went sour, sometimes even bringing the banks to bankruptcy. Poor banking decisions have existed since the beginning of the industry, and must be and are being used to define better procedures.

In the Western countries, billions of dollars worth of loans are made to ordinary individuals against their signatures alone. Every household has credit cards, personal loans and overdraft facilities which are not based on collateral, but instead based on the borrower's character, past credit experience, stability in their job, etc.

Further, any entrepreneur without capital but with bright ideas can put together a syndicate of financiers who specialize in taking risks on ideas and persons, rather than on collateral. In fact some of the main advances in industrial electronics and genetics in the past 20 years have been started by good engineers who were backed by venture capitalists, and in which both the engineer and the venture capitalist made a great deal of money. Of course for each successful venture more than 10 fail, and the venture capitalists lose their money. Venture capital is a highly specialized form of investment, which demands very good business analysis, marketing savvy, and luck. It seems that Islamic banks would do well to look into this, and learn from the venture capital firms. Venture capital is organized by individuals investing their own money, and by investment banks investing their money and their clients' money, and also by mutual funds which attract depositors because of their positive track record.

Islamic banks must be just as eager to protect their net worth as regular banks, and therefore the Islamic banks will assess the risk in a manner very similar to that of a regular bank. The Islamic bank will assess the reputation of the borrower, the use of the funds, the profitability of the account, and the overall chance of seeing the funds returned.

One of the ironies of Islamic banking has been the total lack of enthusiasm of the Saudi Arabian Monetary Agency for this new banking system. SAMA, after years of hesitancy, has only considered allowing two private groups to operate Islamic banks in the kingdom: Al Rajhi Company for Currency and Exchange in Riyadh, and Al Rajhi Islamic Investment Banking company in Jeddah. Both groups operate the largest money changing offices in the kingdom and when SAMA tried to take control of all such business, they thought of converting them into publicly-held Islamic banks. In fact these two companies have yet to receive approval to operate as Islamic banks. In order to float their shares they need a royal decree, which at the time of writing has not yet been finalized, although it has been pending for three years. They also need a decree from SAMA allowing them to be banks, which also has not yet been issued — SAMA waiting probably for the royal decree to be signed.

As the two Al-Rajhi groups are the largest and best regarded money changers in Saudi Arabia, the delays in obtaining the proper decrees are not thought to be because of concern about management or availability of capital. Certainly one of the factors which has rendered SAMA cautious was that the thrust of Islamic banking was carried by Prince Mohammed Al Faysal, who is a controversial figure and does not appear to carry a great deal of credibility in Saudi Arabia. Within the Saudi government there may also be a concern that Islamic banks, by using the name of Islam, could spread rapidly in all strata of the population, and rapidly become a major financial force in the kingdom. A large and powerful Islamic bank in Saudi could become an embarrassment to SAMA, the employees of which have been well trained in the traditional banking procedures of the West and which makes its large investments only in interest-bearing instruments. SAMA may not feel it could control a financial movement bearing the name of God in a country like Saudi Arabia. In a country where the ministry of finance (through SAMA and other institutions) controls all the activities of the economy with a tight hand, it could render the implementation of the government's directives very difficult.

In Kuwait, the only Islamic bank was the Kuwait Finance House.

KFH was established in 1979, with a capital of KD 10 million, eventually increased to KD 35 million, of which the government of Kuwait had 49 per cent. It has provided all kinds of Islamic banking services: Ijara, Musharaka, and Murabaha. Its main activity however has been the Murabaha, in which it has built itself some renown as financing real estate businesses and shares in Kuwait. The *Financial Times* reported on 25 February 1986 that KFH had a portfolio of KD 438 million in land investments, which, if adjusted to real values after the problems in Kuwait since August 1982, could easily bring the net worth of the banks to a large negative figure. Hence it is not surprising to find that in spite of reported profits of US$ 95 million in 1984, the government of Kuwait had to increase its stake in the company to 90.5 per cent,[10] and change the management.

Most of the products created by the Islamic banks do not differ substantially from those of regular banks. The Ijara is extremely close to leasing and, although the wording may differ, the costs and modus operandi are the same. The Bai-Muajjal and Bai-Salam are futures contracts, or swaps, in which the interest element may not be mentioned but is indeed strong. The Musharaka, in final analysis, will not differ from any letter of credit negotiation, with the bank paying at presentation of documents and creating an overdraft account for the borrower. The Murabaha is quite similar to a floating of shares by a venture capital firm. Again we must repeat that the element of risk which is shared in Islamic banking is equally shared in normal banks, and the analysis of each loan and investment is done accordingly.

The products of the Islamic banks appear to be too much of a disguised version of the products of the regular banks. At a time of Islamic revival it is understandable that many Islamists wish to show that a financial system established according to their interpretation of the word of God is viable in the modern world. However it may be that the type of business so far undertaken by the Islamic institutions cannot really succeed if it is to remain a parody of banking.

It is also imperative that the Islamic banks are controlled. In Pakistan and Iran the Islamic banks are under the control of the central banks, and hence are not totally free to play with the depositors' money. In the case of multinational Islamic banks such as Dar Al Mal, there are no ultimate controls. Perhaps an institution like the Islamic Development Bank should be given a role of general controller of all Islamic institutions, with real power to control the figures, the investments, profits and managements of each institution. Such a type of ultimate control would certainly develop a sense of trust among the potential customers of Islamic banks, and also among the non-Islamic financial companies in the world.

It would indeed be naive for the pioneers of Islamic banking to feel that special exceptions should be made to allow them to operate as banks in the Western world if they insist on having no protection for the depositors' money, under the pretext that it is un-Islamic to do so. The central banks of the world did not develop their regulation on capital adequacy out of Christian or Judaic religious fervor, but out of experience. Mr Schotta, Deputy Secretary for Arabian Peninsula Affairs at the US Department of Treasury, in his speech to the Islamic Banking conference in New York in 1985 said:

Protecting the public's interest, as both depositors and borrowers is the raison d'etre for our existing banking practices and regulations . . . During the 1929-1933 period alone, over 100,000 banks ceased to exist. Most simply failed. Many depositors lost their life savings, and the financial system was thrown into chaos by the resulting sharp contraction of the money supply, with the attendant micro dislocations and personal tragedy.

Following these events, it became obvious to bank regulators and lawmakers, that the psychological certainty of the value and accessibility of a depositor's capital would provide the stability necessary to avoid runs on the banking system . . .

The US banking system has specifically sought to insulate depositors from risk, while requiring banks to operate in a manner that minimizes the risk to the institutions themselves. US banking regulations require that for a branch of a foreign entity to function as a retail bank in the US, that is to accept deposits from the public, FDIC insurance is required.

A bank operating procedure which specifically passes investment risk to the depositor appears to run directly counter to the intent of FDIC standards for insurability . . . [a] bank must have an adequate capital base to provide a reasonable cushion against losses . . . [a] bank must be adequately supervised by established bank regulatory authorities.[11]

Islamic banking lends itself to investment and merchant type banking. The Mudaraba, which has been the subject of some abuse, as mentioned above, is also the best vehicle for risk sharing, and real development contribution to the various economies. In order to develop these activities, the Islamic institutions must manage to weed out the swindlers and the poor managers. Perhaps a quick way to learn would be for the large Islamic groups to buy directly large well known investment and merchant banks, which emphasize, as many do today, venture capital, floating of shares on the stock markets, advisory services to corporations and other types of fee income. At any rate the Islamic banks will have to greatly improve their management. They need to develop good capacity to evaluate projects. If Mudaraba is to become a trusted means of investment, the funding of projects like the gold mines of Tanzania, the funding of land speculation in Kuwait, or the financing of large speculation in foreign exchange and gold must stop.

Already new concepts are beginning to appear which undoubtedly will develop. Kleinwort Benson, a very long established English firm, is floating Islamic bonds; Alef Bank, a small Arab-owned institution in Paris is floating mutual funds to the Arab 'gastarbeiters' in France; and Al Baraka Investment Company in Bahrain appears to be more involved in investing its own money than that of its depositors. The Islamic banks could become a major force in the financial world as well as around the Arabian Gulf when they decide not to consider themselves as commercial banks, but as investment banks and venture capital firms, and when they accept tight regulations and disclosure of their operations.

NOTES

1. *Middle East Money*, vol. 1, no. 2, May 1985, p. 15.

2. *Arab Banking and Finance*, November 1984, p. 2.

3. S.H. Homood, *Islamic banking*, Arab Information, London, 1985, p. 225.

4. Ibid., pp. 224-8.

5. Ziauddin Ahmad, 'The present state of the Islamic finance movement', in *The impact and role of Islamic banking in international finance: issues and prospects*, a conference of the US Arab Chamber of Commerce, 28 June 1985, New York, pp. 40-2 of the proceedings.

6. S.H. Homood, 'Islamic banking: limited knowledge restrains progress', article in *Arab banking and finance handbook*, Falcon Press, Bahrain, 1985, p. 102.

7. S.H. Homood, *Islamic banking*, p. 240.

8. Ziauddin Ahmad, 'The present state of the Islamic finance movement', p. 57.

9. S.H. Homood, 'Islamic banking: limited knowledge restrains progress', p. 103.

10. *Middle East Economic Digest*, vol. 28, no. 33, p. B4.

11. Charles Schotta, 'Islamic banking in the US: regulatory issues', in *The impact and role of Islamic banking in international finance: issues and*

prospects, a conference of the US Arab Chamber of Commerce, 28 June 1985, New York.

6

The Other Components of the Gulf Financial Markets

The resultant of all the forces that make a market add to much more than the sum of its various components. They create a life form of their own which breeds upon itself, and develops around most of the obstacles that may be placed to contain it.

In the main financial centers of the world, such as London or New York, the commercial banks and the central banks lend and borrow from each other, the large industrial and service firms issue commercial papers which are constantly bought and sold between all the market players. The investment banks arrange for flotation of shares on the stock markets and whenever necessary underwrite the issues. The investment banks borrow from the public and from the other banks. The insurance companies also interrelate very closely in the markets. They receive funds from the public, manage pension funds, and place funds in the banks, and the investment banks, or themselves lend to certain sectors of the economy. Their money is both in addition to and in competition with that of the banks. There are leasing firms, factoring companies, mortgage companies, second mortgage firms, etc.

Each of the numerous actors in the markets has developed over the centuries according to the needs of some niche in the market which needs special knowledge. All these companies borrow from the public, from the banks and from each other to re-lend to the public, the banks and each other. Dominating the markets are the central banks which exercise their controls by regulations and placing or taking funds from the financial systems.

In the Arabian Gulf the inter-relationship does not yet fully exist. There are a variety of players: the central banks, the commercial banks, the Islamic banks, some investment banks and companies, a few insurance companies, and the money changers. However, they do not yet deal together to any great extent. The commercial banks have been the pioneers in this area. They place funds in each others' treasuries, which, as has been seen, gave birth to the Bahrain market. They share loans made to private firms and government entities in the area.

The central banks also receive funds from the banks, but very seldom place funds in them — they prefer to make deposits in the large Western banks. Funds are placed in London or New York because they are deemed to be safer politically and economically than those placed in the Gulf banks. On the other hand, if some of this money was placed in local banks it could in turn be used by those banks to place among themselves, in the economies of the region or outside, and with other financial players in the markets. In short the central banks appear more concerned to protect their countries' money, rather than develop financial markets which in turn would develop the economies of the Gulf countries. The argument for security is, of course, well founded. The oil wealth will not last forever, and the funds earned by the Arabian nations should be invested wisely for future generations. Kuwait has seen to this more than any other oil producing nations and through KIA, KIO, KFTCIC, etc., has invested large amounts in the industries of the Western nations. Kuwait, as was discussed in detail earlier, has also invested enormous amounts in banks in the Gulf region. This support of the banks however did not come from a desire to develop a market, which in turn would have helped develop the economy, but rather to save the banks from bankruptcy. For its part, SAMA places no deposits in Gulf or other Arab institutions except in banks which it controls totally or partially, such as Gulf International Bank in Bahrain or Saudi International Bank in London.

THE MONEY CHANGERS

In the Arabian Gulf, the non-bank financial players have acted very much like the central banks. They mainly dealt from south to north. The large money changers have used the Western banks to place their extra funds. They trade in commodities with Western banks and investment houses. The money changers, who were the original bankers to the region, are still active. They are nevertheless under great pressure and their days appear to be numbered. Their environment has changed and not all of them have been able to adapt. It also appears that they have not been able to digest the oil boom.

The job of money changer is not an easy one. Even when it means only to receive one currency from a haji or a merchant, change it into the local riyal or dinar and reverse a similar transaction, the money changer has a risk in holding a number of currencies for long periods of time, with potential losses on the the value of each one of them. Before the 1970s, the lack of competition allowed for healthy profit margins which permitted the changers to build a cushion against potential ups and downs in their inventory of currencies. In modern times, competition came with the development of the banks. The profit cushion was whittled away, and the changers had to increase their services to customers.

The main services rendered are spot foreign exchange of all kinds of currencies, even non-convertible currencies, and sales of drafts in foreign currency to expatriate workers or travellers at a better price than those given by banks. Some large changers also provide loans, checking accounts, and letters of credit — in fact acting very much like banks. Some changers even act as semi-investment bankers, providing capital to businesses or using their connections to place shares in various ventures. In Kuwait and Saudi the large money changers have become major dealers in commodities. They deal in gold and silver, in the tradition of their trade, but are also major buyers of wheat, sugar, and rice. Many are also active in the real estate and the share markets. In Saudi Arabia, Abdel Qawi Bamaoudeh has become the largest wheat buyer in the Middle East. The Al Amoudis became the largest importers of rice, controlling an estimated 60 per cent of the market, mainly through their own brand Um Al Khair. In Kuwait, Abul Hassan was a major actor in the stock market. Saleh Rajhi in Riyadh became one of the largest land owners in the kingdom. He was also a pioneer of investment banking. Any businessman needing capital to start an industrial venture could go to Rajhi and if the project appealed to him he would provide most of the capital against 50 per cent of the equity. Rajhi Establishment would also provide the necessary working capital and long-term loans for the company. The cost to the businessman could be very high since once involved with his backer he could not shop around for cheaper sources of financing. However this venture capital activity by Rajhi gave birth to some small-scale industries which were the precursors to the much larger industrial developments that took place after 1974.

The money changers gave birth to an interesting international currency trade, which continues today. The main changers in Jeddah at the time of Haj find themselves with all manner of currency in cash: Syrian pounds, Egyptian pounds, Iraqi dinars, Nigerian nairas, etc.

Each currency is handled differently. The Egyptian pounds are taken in suitcases back to Cairo, where they are exchanged for US dollar bills which are then carried back to Jeddah by air and sold to pilgrims and Egyptian workers who, in turn, take them back to Egypt. The Syrian pounds are sold to the numerous Saudis who travel to Damascus during the summer months. In fact the demand for Syrian pounds can be so strong that pounds are flown in from Beirut. The Syrian currency is smuggled out of Syria by the merchants and often also by government institutions forced to circumvent government regulations to finance the imports of non-essential goods. A large volume of Far Eastern currencies and US dollars are sold to East Asian institutions and exchanged for gold which in turn is carried back to Jeddah regularly by trusted carriers. Other currencies are flown to Basel for exchange in specialized Swiss institutions.

In their fight for market share with the banks the money changers have a major advantage. They are not subject to the control of the monetary agencies and central banks. They can therefore be much more aggressive in their foreign exchange positions. They also do not have to place interest-free deposits with the central banks to abide by reserve requirements. Hence, their costs of funds are lower than those of the banks. They also tend to work out of very old offices and often operate with underpaid staff, so that their overheads are minimal. Their lower costs allow them to charge their customers lower fees on the services, such as personal drafts in a foreign currency. The money changers also provide services which no other institution will provide. They will exchange most currencies at very good rates, but will also accept restricted currencies, even roubles, albeit at a substantial discount. They often will cash personal checks from banks abroad. These services are provided to both small and large customers with a minimum of paperwork, thereby making the money changers the favorites of the public in international money dealings.

Unfortunately, the lack of supervision has brought some abuses, at the expense of their customers. In Bahrain for example, a well known money changer, Mohammed Al Mahrouz, went bankrupt, thereby leaving some of his customers with worthless foreign currency drafts drawn on his accounts in foreign banks. This kind of problem normally hurts the small customer. Many of Al Mahrouz's customers in Bahrain were Indian and Pakistani laborers with wages of BD 40 to BD 1000 per month (US\$ 1,200 to 3,000 per year), who were trying to repatriate their meager earnings at the best possible cost. In his normal course of business Al Mahrouz would issue a draft on, say any bank in India, which would honor the draft upon presentation. The Indian bank would have an account in the name of Al Mahrouz from which it would pay the funds due under the draft. If the money changer had long-standing relationships with the Indian bank the latter would pay the holder of the drafts whether or not the money changer had any funds in his account with them. However if the account was too often left in overdraft, the bank would sooner or later accept to pay only if cash was in the account or cancel the account altogether. In the case of Al Mahrouz, the banks in the sub-continent refused to pay when the accounts were not provisioned by fresh cash, while he continued selling his drafts in Bahrain. Things were made worse for some of the small customers who held on to a number of drafts thinking they would cash them all together once back home. After these problems in November 1984 the government made the Bahrain Monetary Agency responsible for the supervision and licensing of the Bahraini money changers.

All the major money changers maintain extensive relationships with the major banks. They need large foreign exchange lines of credit to trade their daily positions, as well as large treasury lines to be able to pay their customers at maturity of the foreign exchange contracts, and at times when their deposits do not match the maturity of their debt. This type of activity is similar to that of all the banks with each other. In the case of money changers, however, it has often been very difficult to decipher the changer's money from his customer's. Typical of this situation is the bankruptcy of Jawad and Haider Abulhassan in Kuwait. Abulhassan was founded in 1940, and had built an excellent reputation among money changers. It had developed relationships with a number of well-known international banks from which it was borrowing both short-term and medium-term money. In early 1985 Abulhassan defaulted on payments due to varioius banks. The total debt outstanding was around KD 55 million (US$ 183 million). It appears that the losses which brought about the bankruptcy were mainly due to the company's

> secondary role to act as the holding company for the family's investments. It was the latter function which led it into severe dif-ficulties as the steep decline in the value of its local portfolio after the end of 1982 forced it to rely increasingly on short-term money market lines of credit.[1]

The company was hurt by massive investment on the Souk Al Manakh, and possibly by large foreign exchange positions and positions in precious metals which went the wrong way. The government eventually intervened to protect the small clients, who were repaid, and the banks which had extended short-term lines to the company. Some of the medium-term creditors however are still battling to obtain some payment. The problems of the money changers in Kuwait led to a review of the industry by the Central Bank. The Central Bank was asked to review 79 money changing establishments and decide on whether or not to grant them a license to continue operating.[2]

Outside the Arabian Gulf, one of the best-known money changers, Rizk and Saliba Rizk of Amman in Jordan, went into bankruptcy in May 1986 and Saliba Rizk committed suicide. Again the problem of the Jordanian establishment was the permeability of the private accounts of the family with those of the establishments and of the customers. The Rizks had very large positions in foreign exchange and precious metals which turned sour, so that the establishment was not able to meet its commitments to its depositors and customers. The Rizks were the most respected money changers in Jordan, and well known throughout the Arab world. Their demise will fuel the fires of those who are pushing for more control of these establishments.[3]

SAMA has traditionally been wary of the money changers. In December 1981, after the collapse of the Abdullah Al Rajhi establishment (which was described in Chapter 3), SAMA announced a series of measures to bring the money changers under its control. All money changers were required to apply to SAMA to obtain a license to trade in foreign exchange. Their license would be issued only for three years. They would have to keep a minimum of SR 2 million at SAMA, interest free, plus an additional SR 500,000 per branch. They would not be allowed to make loans, take regular deposits or issue checkbooks. They would however be free to apply to SAMA for bank status.[4] Considering that SAMA has not issued a new bank license since its founding, the money changers are probably not excited at the prospect of applying.[5]

Saleh Al Rajhi, the largest of all the changers, has announced his intention to turn his establishment into an Islamic bank. Rajhi's relatives in Jeddah announced a similar plan to start a publicly-owned Islamic financial group. Although most literature on Islamic banks shows that these two entities are established, the fact is that no license has yet been issued — four years after the first requests were made to SAMA. On the other hand it also appears that the SAMA regulations on the money changers were never implemented and that the money changers are still operating as they always have.

The money changers do seem to have strong backing in the conservative circles in Riyadh, hence blocking most of the efforts of

SAMA to bring them to heel. On the other hand they do not have enough clout to impose their entering the market through the guise of Islamic banking, which SAMA and the ministry of finance seem to view with great wariness. Therefore, for the time being the future status of the Saudi money changers is somewhat in limbo. However, even if the authorities are not immediately successful in bringing about these changes, it is likely that many changers will lose customers who are worried by the way their funds are mixed with the changers' family funds and invested in gold, silver, shares, grain, futures, and what-not. The banks are more expensive and the services often not as good, but the customers do know that they have the safety of an ultimate backer, the Saudi government through SAMA, if the banks fail. SAMA may be forced to play a waiting game with the changers, but decisions will eventually have to be made. It is likely that both parties feel that time is playing in their favor. The money changers may feel that sooner or later a more traditional leadership will emerge in Saudi which will confirm them in their role of traditional bankers. SAMA on the other hand would be justified to feel that in the present difficult economic environment, the unregulated and unsupported changers will face other major crises. Certainly, a few of the very major changers in Saudi, especially in Jeddah, are very pressed, because of mismanagement and speculation in commodities. Should another of the changers fail, SAMA will be vindicated and be able to push for its regulation of the industry.

In the end, it appears that the money changers are a vanishing breed. Sooner or later they will be brought under control by the monetary authorities, who may have political motives to do so but are also genuinely worried about protecting the customers. They will, therefore, have to contend with reserve requirements, reporting, computerized systems (which some, like Saleh Al Rajhi, have already implemented) — and altogether much higher overheads. They will also be forced by the authorities to divide the customers' money from the owners'. The changers' speculative investment made with other people's money is by far the most profitable aspect of money changing. If the Rajhis, Kakis, Bamaoudeh, et al. were solely restricted to foreign exchange, they probably would not remain in business. Indeed, in this time of electronic transfers, same day values on funds and wild swings in currencies, they would have to charge large spreads on their deals to cover their costs and risks, making them less competitive than the banks.

THE INSURANCE COMPANIES

The insurance companies in the Arabian Gulf play a very modest role in the financial markets. There are 18 insurance companies in Bahrain alone. However, these firms do not appear to do much more than act as brokers for the larger and more efficient English and American insurance companies.

The local companies mainly insure automobiles and personal liabilities, home theft and fire. In Bahrain there are only four locally-owned companies which underwrite the local policies: the Bahrain Investment Company, Al Ahlia Insurance Co., the National Insurance Company, and Bahrain-Kuwait Insurance Co. (BKIC). In 1984 BKIC, the largest of the four firms, had a total premium income of US\$ 1.6 million for net profits of US\$ 441,500 on a total capital of US\$ 3.2 million.[6]

There are several sizeable brokers, mainly in Saudi Arabia and Kuwait, who sell the policies of various Western insurance companies to insurees around the region. The market is enormous, and will remain so, in spite of the decline in oil prices. The oil industry is certainly the largest user of insurance. In Saudi alone the market was estimated, depending on the source, to generate premiums between US\$ 500 million and US\$ 2 billion.[7] In fact the projects are so large that Aramco self-insures its projects for up to US\$ 10 million and even self-insures its own aeroplanes. In 1984 the Gulf Cooperation Council in Riyadh published a report quoted by *MEED* estimating premiums at US\$ 1 billion of which 30 per cent covered hull and cargoes, 22 per cent contractors, 20 per cent cars and commercial transport, 15 per cent workers' compensation, 10 per cent fire, 3 per cent miscellany. This estimate does not seem to include the premiums paid for oil-related installations, except shipping, which could increase the estimate by a further 50 per cent.

Insurance in Saudi is a sensitive subject. A well-known Saudi lawyer said: 'insurance has somehow got involved with notions of banking interest. It also deals with eventualities such as acts of God and details of prediction. That is the problem.'[8] More specifically Kamal Nasr, in his book on Saudi laws and taxation, simply states that: 'There is no law governing insurance in the kingdom. The Saudi rules based on the Islamic law Shari'a prohibits the engagement in insurance specially life insurance.'[9] Certainly the religious feeling stirred by the notion of insurance has rendered life insurance unknown in the kingdom; however it has not stopped liability, and all other types of insurance are sold quite openly. The insurance companies even insure the 'blood money' which has to be paid in the case of involuntary manslaughter, for example in an automobile accident. Nevertheless the negative atmosphere has not given much incentive to local companies to underwrite policies locally except the smallest policies.

There are 150 companies and brokers operational in Saudi Arabia, of which only six are of some importance. The largest one is Arab Commercial Enterprises, owned by the Olayans in partnership with a UK broker, Sedgwick Forbes.[10] The other five majors are also in close relationship with large European and American insurance companies and brokers.

In spite of the tremendous volumes of premiums gathered in Bahrain, there is only one sizeable local insurance company, the Arab Insurance Group (ARIG) which is owned by the governments of Kuwait, Libya, and the UAE. Although the declared capital is US$ 3 billion, the paid-up capital of the company is only US$ 150 million. ARIG is a re-insurance company. This means that although ARIG may issue some policies directly, its main role is to take shares of insurance issued by other firms, whether local or international. Upon its foundation, and at the sight of its enormous declared capital, ARIG was viewed as a potential competitor to Lloyd's of London. The foundation of ARIG came at the time when Lloyd's temporarily suspended its coverage of ships sailing up the Arabian Gulf because of the Iran-Iraq war. Many felt that ARIG was meant to provide the coverage which Lloyd's had cancelled. Most policies covering shipments of petroleum have to be for US$ 50 million or more so that when the paid-in capital remained at US$ 150 million ARIG failed to make a dent in the market of the region. Undoubtedly this is partly due to its ownership which renders the dealings with ARIG perhaps suspicious to the large Saudi government-owned entities. However, the capital of ARIG is also too small to provide sizeable re-insurance packages, which are absolutely necessary to cover profitably part of the hundreds of millions of dollars of policies fought for at very low margins by the main insurance companies through their local brokers.

ARIG seems to have had substantial management turnover since its creation in 1981, which did not help its market penetration. Finally, since the profits of insurance companies come more from their management of funds than purely from the premiums, which are mostly absorbed by the payments on losses, an insurance company is traditionally an investor in the local economies. In the United States, they provide private placements to industry, which pay more than regular loans. In Europe, as well as in the US, they get involved in large real estate loans and investments, for others and for their own account.

ARIG however does not seem to have been involved in the local economies. This lack of activity is both a blessing and a problem. If ARIG had been involved in the Kuwait stock exchange or the real estate market, it would have lost its capital in less than two years. Thus, ARIG's conservatism helped the company but ARIG could also have been involved in loans to industry or subordinated loans to banks which would have helped the economies and the financial markets to develop.

THE INVESTMENT COMPANIES

In the more sophisticated markets of Kuwait, investment companies rapidly became important players in the financial markets. The investment companies were dominated by three leaders: the Kuwait Foreign Trading, Contracting and Investment Company (KFTCIC), the Kuwait Investment Company SAK (KIC), and the Kuwait International Investment Company (KIIC). The three companies, which are often referred to as 'the three Ks', have been very involved in the development of a bond market in Kuwait. They have led a large number of bond issues in all the major currencies and in Kuwaiti dinars. Their main emphasis has been on leading financing for firms outside the Gulf area and dealings have been with financial institutons in London and New York. As such their involvement in the financial markets in the region remained quite small until they started intervening in the stock market, on order from the Kuwaiti government, to provide support to the share prices.

KFTCIC and KIC, which are the two largest of the three Ks are respectively 94.86 per cent and 64.05 per cent government-owned. KIIC is 24.48 per cent government-owned, and the government has a very strong say in its management. In the past few years the three Ks have had to move away from their position as investment banks to rescuer of the Kuwaiti economy. In the process, however, as can be seen from the table on p. 96, their profitability has totally disappeared.

The two government-owned investment companies have been forced to accept the risk of some of the major stock market speculators in the Souk Al Manakh. KIC advanced KD 105 million and KFTCIC KD 312 million to a total of 17 individuals or firms secured by total assets covering less than half the value of the loans. These loans allowed the 17 investors to avoid bankruptcy and repay a great number of their creditors, and in turn help avoid the latter's bankruptcies.[11]

Table 6.1: The three Ks, 1982-4 (KD million)

Total assets	1984	1983	1982
KIC	304.3	332.5	362.2
KFTCIC	847.4	919.3	787.1
KIIC	208.4	211.5	181.9
Net profits (losses)			
KIC	(32.3)	(19.9)	7.0
KFTCIC	(26.4)	4.8	9.8
KIIC	(10.7)	3.1	8.5

Source: *MEES,* vol. 28, no. 40, p. B2.

The investments made by KIC and KFTCIC were certainly very public spirited, but would have been unthinkable for privately-owned firms. They increased the companies' reliance on government funds to finance the purchases and brought profits down to the level seen above. Further, the real levels of profits are probably much lower than presently shown. Indeed, it is unlikely that the companies have totally marked down the value of their investments in the various Kuwaiti companies along with their value on the stock exchange. In the very long run, however, the investments could prove relatively profitable once the economies in the region start improving. Nevertheless, the salvaging operation mounted by the investment companies is a far cry from the aggressive bond issues and loan syndications which they led between 1977 and 1983.

KFTCIC, which was started in 1965, was very active in the international loan syndications. In the early years it mostly arranged loans to other Arab states such as Algeria, and eventually led syndications to countries like Yugoslavia. Between 1977 and 1983 KFTCIC arranged US$ 1,853 million of loans, of which 31.5 per cent were to Arab states, 17.7 per cent to Western Europe, 16.5 per cent to Asia and 34.3 per cent to all other areas.[12] KFTCIC also became very active in other markets. It became a large issuer of straight dollar bonds, floating rate notes (FRNs), Kuwaiti dinar bonds, US dollar convertible bonds and zero coupon US dollar bonds.

KIC, although smaller than KFTCIC, was much larger in the bond markets in numerous currencies, such as US dollars, French francs, Deutschemarks and Kuwaiti dinars. KIC was also a major player in the floating rate notes market. It developed a very good reputation in these fields and was able to develop a customer base of very high quality companies and entities. In 1980 KIC led issues for General Motors Acceptance Corporation, the European Coal and Steel Community and the Bank of Tokyo, clients which only work with firms of the calibre of Morgan Guaranty or Solomon Brothers.

KIIC, to a lesser extent, was also very successful in developing a good customer base and managed to lead syndications for the Banque Française du Commerce Exterieure and All Nippon Airways.

Table 6.2: Total issues by the three Ks between 1979 and 1983 (US$ million)

	$ Bonds	$ FRNs	KD Bonds	Other	Total
KIC	668.21	246.64	274.48	436.32	1,625.65
KFTCIC	203.14	69.32	202.84	305.15	780.45
KIIC	184.84	133.03	269.24	408.11	995.22
Total	1,056.19	448.99	746.56	1,149.58	3,401.32

Source: Mehran Nakhjavani, *Arab banks and the international financial markets*, MEPEP, Nicosia, 1983.

The products offered and managed by the three Ks were very sophisticated — on a par with those offered by the main Western institutions. It is most interesting that the KD denominated bonds became as large as they did. The Kuwaiti dinar is a small currency with no depth or international basis. There is no trade denominated in dinars, and no foreign banks keep their reserves in dinars. Hence the whole idea of issuing Kuwaiti dinar bonds was for the Kuwaiti institutions to sell down the bonds to the Kuwaiti public, or to institutions which had the ability to borrow Kuwaiti dinars from the Kuwaiti institutions, whether banks or investment companies. From the borrowers point of view, issuing paper in their name in Kuwaiti dinars was of interest as their cost would be way below the normal US dollar rate of this period. The borrowers ranged from various nation states such as the Philippines, Ireland, Iceland, Mexico, Panama, to large firms such as Mitsubishi, BNP, Union Pacific etc. Typically, the issues were relatively small, between 5 and 10 million dinars (US$ 17 to 35 million) with maturities of 5 to 10 years, and coupons between 7 and 10 per cent — a very attractive cost compared to dollar rates of 11 to 14 per cent during the same period.

However, issuing bonds to foreign borrowers in dinars implies that this currency will be easily available to the borrowers when they need to pay the dividends and redeem the bonds. It also implies that a secondary market for the bonds inside and outside Kuwait should develop. Hence, issuing bonds denominated in Kuwaiti dinars rendered Kuwait susceptible to the internationalization of its currency.

Although the investment banks may have supported an internationalization of the dinar, the Kuwaiti government was not necessarily keen on seeing a Eurodinar market develop in Europe or in Bahrain. The currency restrictions on placing of dinars outside Kuwait in 1978 was an indication that the Central Bank was aware of the problems inherent in the development of a Eurodinar. If the dinar had become easily available and at a good interest rate, there would have been a disintermediation which would have led to large increases in dinar interest rates, or changes in currency values, with only little control by the Kuwaiti authorities. On the one hand, the government-controlled investment companies were eager to develop a new instrument in the markets which would put them among the world's financial leaders. On the other hand Kuwait is a small country with a very limited currency pool, in terms of world banking, and the dinar bond market was short-lived. After the problems of the Souk Al Manakh, and the decrease in oil petroleum, the dinar issues more or less disappeared from the international markets.

Other problems also plagued the development of the Kuwaiti investment companies. Banque Bruxelle Lambert and Solomon Brothers were placed on the Arab boycott in 1981 and 1983 respectively. Since Solomon ranked second and BBL tenth in the number of issues managed in 1981, it was very difficult for the Kuwaiti companies to issue bonds which could not receive the support of these two key institutions, and the three Ks could not participate in any of the numerous issues led by the boycotted institutions. Further it created a feeling of unreliability among both customers and financial institutions. How could a large AAA-rated firm mandate any Arab institutions to underwrite and issue its paper, if the Arab bank was not able to deal with the major players in the world markets? Not to mention the legal problems which the US firms could have if deemed to support the Arab boycott of Israel. Eventually both BBL and Solomon were removed from the blacklist but the damage was done. In *Arab banks and the international financial markets* Nakhjavani sees a parallel between the problem of boycott and the slow down in Arab penetration of the bond market after 1981.[13]

The Central Bank of Kuwait shows in its economic charts that there are 27 investment companies in Kuwait, with total assets of KD 1.8 billion in 1984, down to KD 1.6 billion in 1985.[14] Since in

1984 the total assets of the three Ks was KD 1.3 billion, the 24 other companies share KD 500 million in assets. Most of the other investment companies of Kuwait are privately-held firms, such as Kuwait Financial Center or Al-Ahlia Investment Company, which have sustained very large losses in the stock market crash, and a number of them are in the process of being liquidated by government order.

In Bahrain, the Kuwaiti financiers had started a number of Exempt Companies (EC), mainly to have shares to sell on the Souk Al Manakh in Kuwait. The companies themselves were usually fairly active on the stock exchanges and here again are mostly being liquidated. The six main companies were the Al-Jazira Contracting and Investment Company, the Arab International Development Company, the Pearl Investment Company, the Gulf Investment Company, the Gulf Consolidated Services and Industries Company and the Bahraini-Kuwaiti Investment Group. All were EC companies. Their aggregate net worth declined from US$ 1,019 million in 1982 to US$ 534 million in 1984 (not including a probable negative net worth for Al-Jazira).[15] These companies were covered in the reorganization of the stock markets in Kuwait, and their shares are now mostly owned by the government or one of the government intermediaries such as KFTCIC.

The investment companies had started to become the nucleus of a real market. The three Ks were involved both internationally, and in the Arab world. They were imaginative and tried to develop modern financing techniques. The private investment firms were even more involved in the local markets, buying and selling shares, taking companies public, placing and taking funds in banks, etc. Unfortunately, it all went too fast, too soon. A low-key approach under more control from the Central Bank would have helped the investment companies weather the storms. It would have limited the stock market crash and the overall decrease in liquidity. Again, greed overcame common sense — to the damage of the whole economy.

There were no investment companies similar to the Kuwaiti ones founded in Saudi Arabia. For the record the Arab Investment Company (TAIC) and the Arab Petroleum Investment Corporation (APICORP) should be mentioned. TAIC, which is officially based in Riyadh but is mainly active from its branch in Bahrain, has acted as a wholesale commercial bank. However, TAIC has been limited by its charter to keep its activities to the countries of the Arab League which are its shareholders. This geographical restriction has stopped TAIC from becoming very active in the loan syndication markets and investment banking in the three Ks' style. TAIC, nevertheless, has tried to diversify away from commercial banking and was able to develop a bond and FRN dealing activity in Bahrain where it is a market maker.

APICORP, which is owned by the countries of OAPEC, had not had any significant activity in the financial markets of the region. It has joined and managed a few syndicated loans but it has mainly restricted itself to financing oil-related investments in OAPEC countries outside the Gulf.

In Bahrain, the government has tried to promote the development of non-bank financial institutions. After 1981 BMA allowed the establishment of investment banks. Although there was no minimum capital requirement expressed in the law, the candidates to the Investment Banking License (IBL) were required to start an Exempt Company with a minimum capital of US$ 20 million. The IBLs were also required to keep their leverage below 10 to 1, but in some cases this was raised to 15 to 1. The companies were not encouraged to develop trade finance, but otherwise could arrange long-term, medium-term and short-term financing. They could have a dealing room, which could buy and sell funds from all institutions.

At first it was not quite clear what the difference would be between the regular OBUs and the new IBLs. In fact the OBUs are allowed to do any and all of the type of business which both commercial and investment banks do. There is no Glass-Steagall type separation of powers between the two types of banks. Most restrictions on the OBUs to avoid investment-type banking originated in the parent country of certain banks such as the American ones, or were due to the lack of investment banking knowledge of the OBUs' staff. Over time, it has appeared that the IBL structure was adopted, successfully, by the Japanese security houses and banks. In the difficult environment of 1986 the Japanese IBLs are growing, while most other institutions are shrinking. Sumitomo Finance (Middle East) EC and Nomura Investment Banking (Middle East) EC, have been faring very well. Their main activities are to sell and trade Japanese securities to the central banks, the investment companies, the banks, and private individuals in the region. The Japanese firms benefit from a tax-free environment and a strong local presence which allows them to make a market for their securities locally without having to refer to Tokyo. With the Japanese yen as strong as it is in 1986, and likely to remain and even become more of a component in the portfolios of the Gulf, the future of the Japanese IBLs is probably very good.

There are other IBLs in Bahrain which have had substantial and continuous success. The Trans-Arabian Investment Bank (TAIB) was at first involved in syndications of regional facilities to international banks. TAIB was very successful in this field, packaging and structuring facilities for companies that had not borrowed from the international banks. This activity has slowed down considerably, after the numerous bankruptcies and liquidations in the region in which banks have lost money. However TAIB has developed other successful activities such as trade finance, and sale of real estate investments.

The Arabian Investment Banking Corporation, mainly known as Investcorp, has developed an expertise in leverage buy-outs of companies in the United States, such as the purchase of Tiffany in New York.

We said earlier that the development of the OBUs in Bahrain was greatly helped by the large incentives which existed in the Saudi riyal/US dollar disintermediation. The large volume of foreign exchange and money market activities brought a number of money brokers to Bahrain. Their activity is to match the demand and supply of currencies and funds by calling banks and corporations. The main firms were RP Martin and Marshall's, both of which have substantial activities in other financial centers in the world. There was also an Arab-owned brokerage firm. However this firm ran into difficulties, and had to be reorganized. A broker normally never takes a position in any currencies or money markets: he is only an intermediary. Consequently, brokers do not have to rely on their capital to cover any potential loss. Their earnings are based on a percentage of the size of each transaction — usually 1/32 per cent on both sides. The money brokers in Bahrain are all English except for United Arab Broking Company. UABC is the successor to another Arab broker which is thought to have done dealings for its own account, as well as for its customers and was not able to cover its losses. The Arab broker, which had been developing rapidly in the late 1970s and was hoping to become one of the world leaders in this field, even opening in London, had to start from scratch with new Arab owners in a difficult market.

There is only one other important player among the privately-owned Gulf financial institutions — the Arab Leasing Company. Arab Leasing was first started as a joint venture between BAII and Arinfi. Arinfi is a very large investment company whose main shareholder is KIIC, and which has invested heavily in real estate in France and in the United States. Arab Leasing developed its business in the region by taking in shareholders from Saudi Arabia and the UAE, where it could rely on the shareholder to hold title to the properties being leased, and thus by-pass the rules of each country against ownership of goods by foreigners. Unfortunately, Arab Leasing suffered considerable losses, especially in Saudi Arabia on equipment finance. Arab Leasing suffered from the unreliability of the legal systems in the region. It could not easily repossess its own equipment, and if repossessed after difficult and expensive battles, could not always resell it in a falling construction market. In 1984 Arinfi took the majority of the shares, by buying out BAII, and brought in Al Baraka group for 20 per cent of the shares.[16]

At this time there are no other major players in the privately-owned financial sector. There is room for more institutions, such as factoring companies, or mortgage companies. However, the market is not likely to engender more firms or get any deeper until the basic commercial laws in the main markets of the region are made somewhat more accommodating to financial institutions.

NOTES

1. *Middle East Economic Survey*, vol. 28, no. 25, p. B1.
2. *Middle East Economic Digest*, 7 December 1985, p. 22.
3. For more information on the Rizk bankruptcy, see *Money*, June 1986.
4. Rodney Wilson, *Banking and finance in the Arab Middle East*, Macmillan, London, 1983, p. 171.
5. In fact the number of banking licenses in the kingdom was actually reduced, when SAMA arranged the merger of the Banque du Liban et d'Outre Mer, the Banque Melli, and United Bank of Pakistan into the Saudi Commercial United Bank under the management of Saudi International Bank of London of which SAMA is the main shareholder.
6. *Middle East Economic Digest*, 'Special Report', October 1985, p. 13.
7. This information was collected from *Arab Banking and Finance*, May 1981 and *Middle East Economic Digest*, July 1985, 'Special Report on Saudi Arabia', p. 51.
8. *Middle East Economic Digest*, 'Special Report on Saudi Arabia', July 1985, p. 51.
9. Kamal S. Nasr, *Business laws and taxation in Saudi Arabia*, Riyadh, 1979, p. 142.
10. *Middle East Economic Digest*, 'Special Report', July 1985, p. 51.
11. *Middle East Economic Survey*, vol. 29, no. 13, p. B3.
12. Merhan Nakhjavani, *Arab banks and the international financial markets*, MEPEP, Nicosia, 1983, pp. 38-9.
13. Ibid., p. 75.
14. Central Bank of Kuwait, *Economic chart book* vol. 7, 1985, Kuwait, pp. 46, 47.
15. *Financial Times*, 'Special section on Bahrain', 22 July 1985.
16. *Middle East Money*, June 1985, p. 13.

7

Government Financial Institutions Other than the Central Banks

In order to promote their policies, the governments in Saudi Arabia, Bahrain and Kuwait have developed institutions which are expected to provide types of financing to the local population that may not have been provided otherwise by the private sector.

The main institutions created by the various governments and which will be discussed here were the Saudi Industrial Development Fund (SIDF), the Agricultural Bank of Saudi Arabia, and the Real Estate Bank, also of Saudi Arabia. Bahrain and Kuwait also had real estate institutions, but their roles were quite minor, and the amounts lent minimal. In Saudi on the other hand, the figures are very large, and obviously the role of the three banks mentioned has been to promote the development of each country according to the views of the Kings, especially King Fahad.

Kuwait and Bahrain have left most of the housing and industrial loans to the private market, which, in both countries, could accept mortgage lending, although not as strictly enforced as in the Western countries. The total loans of the government-owned Kuwait Real Estate Bank, the Industrial Bank of Kuwait and the Credit and Savings Bank totalled about US$ 2 billion, which pales somewhat if compared to the total Saudi disbursements to industry, agriculture, and housing of US$ 234 billion.[1] The agricultural sector is very important to Bahrain, but the government support of agriculture has remained relatively small.

The Saudi Industrial Development Fund was created in 1984 by King Faysal with the specific purpose to finance the development of industrial projects in the kingdom. The minister of finance, with some insight, figured that the fastest way to start a successful operation was to buy management from a Western institution. Sheikh Abal Khail chose to give the contract to the Chase Manhattan Bank. Why Chase was chosen is not obvious, but one can guess that Sheikh Abal Khail felt that since Chase had very large deposits from the kingdom, the minister could put pressure on Chase to give to SIDF its best possible support. By and large, if such was the intent of the minister, he appears to have been quite right. Chase Manhattan quickly went into gear and by December of 1974 had found a general manager, an operations manager, a senior lending officer and a junior lending officer. The staff was rapidly increased so that by March 1975, a full lending team was on the spot. For their part the Saudis provided junior Saudi officers, and a deputy general manager. The start-up capital was SR 500 million.

The priorities of SIDF were quickly defined by the Saudis. In 1974 the problems of infrastructure were enormous, and the government was able to divide the tasks between the private and public sectors. The public sector was responsible for funding and engineering the basic infrastructure, roads, harbors, airports, telephone communications, schools and hospitals. On the other side the government would provide the incentives to the private sector to develop the plants and factories needed to produce the materials necessary to the contractors who were building the government-planned infrastructure. Incentives consisted of cheap energy, communications, land and long-term low-interest finance of industrial projects from SIDF.

The ministry of commerce and industry developed large industrial parks in the main cities of the kingdom. The parks were equipped with proper sewage, electricity, water and roads. The ministry let land in the parks to any properly licensed industry at SR 1 per square meter. SIDF for its part financed 50 per cent of the fixed assets and working capital needs of all projects it approved, and demanded from the investors at least 25 per cent capital. Often investors tried artificially to inflate the costs of the projects so that the loan made by SIDF on 50 per cent of the presented project would cover the capital expected from the shareholders. SIDF was always aware of the practice and in most cases was able to reduce the scope or the price of the projects to ensure proper capitalization by the investors. However the capital to be paid was often borrowed from banks, against the investors' personal guarantees. SIDF's loans are for periods of up to 15 years, with a grace period of up to 5 years, depending on the expected cash flow of the project. The interest costs to the borrowers were 2 per cent at first which eventually was reduced to a nominal fee supposed to repay the costs of the credit reviews.

The largest and most immediate demand in the kingdom was for building materials which were needed for private housing, government ordered infrastructure projects, and privately-owned industries. Until 1975 most of the cement used in Saudi was imported through Jeddah, with a small proportion produced locally in Riyadh and in Jeddah. Cement was imported in bags which required time and labor to handle and added to the large delays in the harbors. The price of imported concrete was at times as high as SR 50 per 100 pound bag. Cement was used for concrete making which was usually mixed on site. Within five years the construction industry was totally revolutionized and progressed 50 years to use very modern processes. SIDF financed cement plant expansions in Riyadh and Jeddah, and bulk delivery plants to be installed in Jeddah, Dammam, and Yanbu. In 1974 total local production of cement was 1 million tons and imports 1.5 million tons. In 1980 production was up to 2.9 million tons and imports up to 10 million. In 1981 production jumped to 4.8 million tons. By 1984 production had reached 8.6 million tons, while import figures not available for 1984 had reached 15.5 million tons in 1983.[2]

Prior to 1974, the quality of construction was very poor: one of the major problems was the quality of sands and aggregate used to mix with the cement to make concrete. Hence the private sector saw an opportunity to make money if it could provide washed sand and aggregates. SIDF obliged and within three years had arranged for the financing of enough plants to meet all the local demand for washed aggregates and sands.

One of the most important building materials was cement blocks which, in Saudi, were mostly used for building private houses. Hence for social reasons it was important to maximize production and quality. However, prices were very high — up to SR 10 per block, even for those of very low quality — and so SIDF went on a cement block plant financing binge. For some six months in 1976, it was approving 1 cement block plant per week. The role of SIDF was not only financial; the fund also provided technical advice through an engineering team. It would only approve projects which were planned so that price would be reasonable and quality greatly improved. By the end of 1976, a series of modern cement block plants had been built and were operational. The price of blocks went from the SR 10 mentioned down to SR 2 — and quality improved considerably.

SIDF also promoted other types of construction materials. A series of red brick plants were built in Jeddah and Riyadh. Near both towns are located large deposits of high quality clays which can be used to make very high quality bricks. Since modern brick-making techniques require minimal labor, but large amounts of energy and clay, these new building blocks were ideal for Saudi Arabia.

The plans for the new industrial towns in Yanbu and Jubail, as well as the immediate demand for quality housing, schools, clinics, and various government buildings in the cities, was partly met by large-scale use of prefabricated housing. The Saudi entrepreneurs were able to bring to life some of the largest plants in the world for prefabricated panels to be used in quick, quality construction. They brought engineering from Europe, labor from the Philippines and Korea, and built and operated the plants with great success. The best case in point is MABCO, owned mainly by Sheikh Omar Aggad, who also managed to develop a number of other very successful industrial ventures in the kingdom. MABCO operates two prefab plants, one in Riyadh and the other in Jubail, and has obtained the largest share of the contracts to build the new Jubail town. The plants are amongst the largest in the world, and have been very profitable.

SIDF financed the extension of two very large asbestos cement pipe plants, the production of which is used to make pressure pipes for water distribution. Also financed in the building materials domain were a very large aluminium extrusion plant, which made the extrusions needed for making windows and doors used in all the buildings in the kingdom, asphalt plants, crushers, truck bodies, and basically all manner of construction supplies. SIDF also funded industrial projects which may not have been directly related to construction but the production of which was driven by demand stemming from the construction boom. A large wall-to-wall carpet and machine-made oriental rugs plant was built in Jeddah, in joint venture with an Italian government-owned company. In each city in the kingdom there were furniture factories built to make office and house furniture. Smaller plants making lamps, industrial curtains and all sorts of decorations were also built.

The peak activity for construction-related loans by SIDF was in 1976 and 1977 when SR 508 million and SR 1,299 million were approved for cement and construction materials alone.[3] Between 1974 and 1984 the total disbursements of SIDF totalled SR 8.5 billion (US$ 2.4 billion) of which 37 per cent went to the cement and construction material industries, financing approximately 3,000 new projects and expansion on existing plants. The balance of the money lent by SIDF, SR 5.3 billion, was on all other types of industry, with emphasis after 1981 on food processing plants: meat packing, dairy plants, soft drinks bottlers, etc.[4] Among the larger industrial projects, the fund financed a large air-conditioner factory in joint venture with Friedrich Corporation, a spiral welded steel pipe-line plant in joint venture with Sumitomo of Japan, and three very large printing plants. In 1986 there were 1,886 factories in the kingdom (from almost none in 1973) which were 28 per cent in the metal transformation industries, 27 per cent in building materials, 16 per cent in food processing, and 14 per cent in the chemical industries.[5]

In 1975 the government quickly became aware that the industrial development of the kingdom as well as the welfare of the people was very dependent on reliable electricity supplies. The government instructed SIDF to start a department within its own organization that would specialize in providing proper engineering advice and financing to bring forth a quick development and standardization of the electricity supplies in the kingdom. There again SIDF was hugely successful, disbursing SR 23 billion between 1975 and 1984 to the power companies. As a consequence, production went from 1 million kWh in 1393 (1973/4) to 31 million kWh in 1403 (1982/3). The 31-fold increase in ten years is in the writer's opinion unmatched anywhere. SIDF hired the large American electrical engineering firm Stone and Webster Engineering Corporation of New York to evaluate the needs of each electricity company and help draw up with the ministry of industry and electricity the guidelines for the integration of the systems in the kingdom. Certainly the fact that Saudi Arabia is the only country in the Arab world with US standards for electricity, i.e. 110 volts, 60 cycles, is due to the American influence. One can perhaps regret the fact that the international standards were not accepted, since it would have removed a barrier to a wider integration of GCC electrical resources in the future. On the other hand most Saudi electrical engineers have been trained by Aramco in the United States, and therefore are more familiar with US standards, and hence could develop the resources faster. Also the distances between population centers are such that needs for an integration of GCC electrical resources are still a number of years away.

SIDF financing of the industrial and electrical sectors was a great success. The large increase in electricity production mentioned above is only one example of its impact. In great part attributable to SIDF are the increases in non-oil gross national product figures. Gross fixed investment in the non-oil private sector went from SR 6.7 billion in 1975 to SR 133.5 billion in 1984 and gross domestic product in constant riyals went from 8.4 billion in 1975 to SR 25.4 billion in 1984.[6]

In the first ten years after the increase in petroleum revenues, the industrialization of the kingdom was very much driven by the construction industry, which accounted for up to 81 per cent of gross fixed investments.[7] After 1984 when most large infrastructure

107

projects were finished and petroleum prices started to decline rapidly, the need for a construction-based industry started to decline very substantially. The very large construction materials plants were no longer so necessary. A major shake out of the industry started to take place leaving only those that were the most efficient. In the immediate future the enormous government pressures to develop the kingdom and encourage the construction industry may not be entirely appreciated by the many entrepreneurs who used and lost their funds in creating plants that fulfilled a temporary need. As is often the case in quickly developing economic sectors, whether it be pork in the EEC, real estate in New York, or cement blocks in Saudi Arabia, a large demand creates high prices and profits for the few first producers. The high profits spur the creation of many producing entities, which eventually come to the market with their production all at the same time. Hence, as prices crash down because of competition, the profits which were being counted upon disappeared, and bankruptcies of the poorly managed and lowly capitalized are common.

SIDF was itself caught in the massive build-up of the economy, and even if it foresaw the difficulties that most of the smaller investors would face, it could not have easily stopped it. Any investor who wished to start a factory had to obtain a license from the ministry of commerce. The license would be issued on the strength of market needs as perceived by the ministry. The perception of the ministry of commerce and industry was based on five-year plans as interpreted by the officials of the ministry. The building boom had been correctly foreseen by both the ministry of commerce and industry and the ministry of planning. The perceptions were further influenced by the daily frustrations encountered by all citizens, including government officials, because of the lack of infrastructure. The political choice was either to place stringent quotas on the issuance of industrial licenses at the risk of delaying the development of the nation by ten years, delaying the alleviation of frustrations by the same period, or to issue enough licenses to create more immediate relief, but at the risk of creating gluts once the main needs were fulfilled. The government obviously chose the latter course, which was implemented with the help of SIDF. As a consequence the country was modernized in ten years, but is now vastly over-equipped with construction industries.

The role of Chase Manhattan Bank in SIDF was most important in the early years. Chase, although not a development bank, was able to provide SIDF with relatively sophisticated analysis techniques, and general management proficiency. Chase's main contribution to the fund was the enthusiasm of most of the staff it attracted, both foreign and Saudi. It was able to imbue entrepreneurial spirit into its loan officers, who evaluated the projects mostly from a commercial feasibility standpoint. This attitude was encouraged by the Saudi managers, who eventually took over the management of the fund. Of course Chase was criticized for using commercial practices for development loans. On the other hand Chase was also under pressure from the government to minimize the losses, and ensure that the government subsidies would not be viewed as hand-outs that would promote the creation of white elephants and in general of inflation. Obviously, the government must have felt that SIDF had some degree of success since its first Saudi general manager became governor of SAMA, and all its first Saudi officers have gone to positions of high responsibility in the government.

SIDF has probably been the most successful development bank in the world. The amounts of disbursement surpass that of any other country. Further, the level of losses has been remarkably low. An officer of the fund mentioned to the writer that the loan losses were below 2 per cent, which is similar to many commercial banks. Of course, and especially in the 1986 environment, many loans have been rescheduled rather than written off, but again this is similar to all commercial banks. Nevertheless, the low level of losses points to the quality of analysis which SIDF brought to its work.

SIDF played a very important role in the economic modernization of the kingdom. It demanded that all applications emphasized management techniques and marketing, and required that firms which obtained loans keep properly audited books. The last point was important in developing the economy since with audited statements, commercial banks could more readily finance the companies. SIDF encouraged the banks to lend medium-term funds to cover the 25 per cent of the projects not covered by SIDF and the capital contribution, including making precedents for joint mortgages on plant and equipment. Eventually mortgages were forbidden to all lenders including SIDF, hence SIDF's attempts to develop medium-term loans by the commercial banks failed.

In spite of the overall success of SIDF, it seems that it failed in one major area. SIDF never really made a special effort to finance the small industries. Indeed, the manpower needed to evaluate and structure a project is similar whatever the size of the project. The management of SIDF was faced with great pressure to show an improvement in the industrialization of the kingdom and an improvement in the quality of the materials produced locally, and so could not divert the time of its officers to small projects. In the long run, however, having a large number of small industries provides depth to the economy and allows the swings in demand and supply to be spread over a larger spectrum of the population. Perhaps the ministry of finance should have asked SIDF to develop a small loan department which would have acted more as a disbursement agent than a thorough analytical group. With a capital of SR 1 billion the small industry department could have financed perhaps 2,000 small industrialists. Of course, losses may have been as high as 50 per cent, but such losses would be very small compared to the overall GNP of the kingdom, and little compared to the vast sums spent on the military.

The next step in the promotion of industry in the kingdom will not be easy for SIDF. The private sector is still expected to fill in the gaps of industrialization. At present this means primarily plants and industries not covered by the government's implementation of the Jubail and Yanbu programs. However, since a number of investors have had their fingers burned once with the sudden recession in the building material industry, the private sector will probably be very careful in investing its money in local projects for fear of another boom-bust situation. Further, with less money going to the private sector because of decreased oil revenues, less is available for venture capital. SIDF can only subsidize the private sector but cannot replace it; hence, if private investments lag, SIDF's role will begin to decline.

The second most important government specialized institution is the Real Estate Development Fund. Its purpose was to provide all citizens with enough money to build a private residence, with loans of up to 25 years at no interest. The fund, in order to encourage repayments, went as far as offering 20 per cent discount to the borrowers who were able to pay the loan instalments on time and a further 30 per cent discount in case of full repayment before maturity. The fund was founded in 1394, but did not manage to make its first loans before 1396/7. Eventually it was able to provide 64,902 loans between 1395 and 1404, for a total of SR 355.6 billion. The loans financed the building of 332,470 private units and 23,133 rental units.[8] The amounts made available by the Real Estate Fund freed the commercial banks from providing mortgage loans to the public. In any case, the banks felt shy of making home loans because of the stigma attached to mortgages in the kingdom.

Finally, there is the government-owned Agricultural Bank. Its role is to promote the development of agriculture with the goal in mind of bringing this desert kingdom to agricultural self-sufficiency. As was the case for SIDF, the government was able to lure the private sector into making large investments with the prospect of easy profits. It instituted a system of handouts that made it difficult to lose money in agriculture.

Any purchases of farm implements such as seeds, tools, water pumps and fertilizers were financed by grants from the Agricultural Bank for 50 per cent of their CIF value, pesticides for 100 per cent, and even imported dairy cows for 50 per cent. Capital expenses of farm development, if approved by the ministry of agriculture, were financed at no interest by the bank for long-term periods of up to 30 years, for a maximum amount of SR 20 million (US$ 5.7 million).[9] Further, the government, having decided to foster self-sufficiency in the agricultural sector, offered to buy all the wheat produced at the equivalent of SR 3,500 per ton (US$ 1,000) corresponding to five times world prices.[10] Eventually the subsidies on wheat production were reduced to bring prices to SR 2,000 per ton (US$ 530), about three times world market prices.[11] High prices coupled with the incentives of the Agricultural Bank made Saudi Arabia a producer of wheat surpluses. By 1984, Saudi Arabia was producing 1.3 million tons of wheat per annum. In 1985 it even started to export at close to world market prices. With the existing squeezes in oil income, such a program is very much a luxury, and the government tried to decrease the incentives. Like the apprentice sorcerer, however, the government found it easier to unleash the production than to stop it, as so many powerful private interests would suffer if subsidies were cut. Further, the enormous development of agriculture is taxing heavily the water resources of the kingdom. Most of the farms are too far from the desalinated supplies and hence must rely on the fossilized water deposits, some 100 to 500 meters deep, depending on location, which cannot be regenerated.

Between 1395/6 and 1403/4, the Agricultural Bank made 165,046 loans for a total of SR 13.339 billion (US$ 3.8 billion). The success of the agricultural policies was undeniable in terms of production. As well as the production of wheat, the kingdom increased its chicken production from 8,105 tons in 1393 to 200,633 tons in 1404, increasing the local production to 55 per cent of total consumption. Production of eggs increased from 114.4 tons in 1393 to 1,761.2 tons in 1404, equivalent to 100 per cent of consumption.[12]

All these industrial and agricultural activities created corollary financial activities as well as investments in warehouses, machinery maintenance, and distribution networks which certainly added a number of new faces to the families which until now had made the economic fabric of the kingdom. The funds disbursed by SIDF, the Real Estate Fund and the Agricultural Bank found their way into the financial systems in Saudi Arabia and in the Gulf.

One of the activities triggered by the agricultural subsidies was bridge-financing of the money payable by the government to the farmers on their wheat crop. This activity was not entirely without risks, since the Agricultural Bank is not managed as professionally as SIDF, and is not under the highly efficient surveillance and management of the Minister of Finance. Certain foreign banks, who undoubtedly knew of the difficulties of perfecting their security, and obtaining redress in the courts, would advance money to a 'farmer' (often a prince or a rich merchant) and apply for payment to the Agricultural Bank. The commercial bank which had lent to a farmer counted on being paid directly by the Agricultural Bank. Unfortunately, the Agricultural Bank is under no obligation and in fact is not permitted to accept the assignment of payments issued by the borrower in favor of a foreign bank. Consequently the farmer could get his payment directly from the Agricultural Bank and repay the commercial bank at his leisure. Hence, some banks have taken substantial losses on this type of activity.

In the case of SIDF, however, numerous activities for the commercial banks were generated because of SIDF's activities. The commercial banks, whether in Bahrain or in Saudi, opened letters of credit to import machinery and raw materials necessary for the projects. The banks could finance the projects themselves and in some cases the capital of the project promoters. Thus, the money originating from the government was multiplied through normal market activities.

There is also a fund which is not much discussed in the literature about the economic development and the financial markets in the region — the Public Investment Fund of Saudi Arabia. This fund is owned by the government and managed by the Ministry of Finance. It was created in 1394 with a capital of SR 600 million. Its mission is to provide equity money for the major development efforts of the government. Originally PIF was expected to invest in large long-term projects such as SABIC's petrochemical, metallurgical and fertilizing plants. Once these projects became profitable, PIF was to sell the shares to the public, in order for the public to have an interest in the development of the country.[13] PIF became one of the main shareholders in Saudia, the airline of the kingdom, Petromin, and SABIC. In fiscal 1403/4 PIF disbursed SR 5.8 billion, raising its total disbursements to SR 49 billion (US$ 14 billion).[14] It is not very clear today whether PIF will ever divest itself of the shares it has in the large firms of the kingdom. The government has floated shares to the public in Saudia and SABIC on top of PIF's contributions. Further, in SAMA's Annual Report of 1404, the PIF contribution is mentioned as being loans rather than equity participations. At any rate, PIF is considered to be part of the ministry of finance; it is housed in the building of the ministry, and headed by one of the deputy ministers of finance.

In spite of some substantial shortcomings, the influence of the Saudi government-owned institutions has been extremely positive. SIDF has been the main support of the industrialization of the kingdom. The Agricultural Bank has helped bring green to the desert and make the country self-sufficient in grains, eggs and poultry. The Real Estate Bank has helped all the citizens obtain decent housing. In view of the difficult legal environment for banks the government institutions are able to lend the long-term funds needed for the development of the industry. The other side of the coin unfortunately is that the development of industry is dependent on the goodwill of the government, and this can make the economy unable to adapt to change.

NOTES

1. These figures were computed from the Central Bank of Kuwait, *Economic Chart Book*, vol. 7, 1985, Kuwait, p. 45, netting out the loans made by Kuwait Finance House mentioned in Chapter 5. The Saudi figures were used by totaling the disbursements of SIDF, PIF, the Real Estate Bank and the Agricultural Bank, using an average exchange rate of SR 3.5 per US$.

2. SAMA, *Annual reports*, 1401, p. 167; 1404, pp. 101, 186.

3. SAMA, *Annual reports*, 1401, pp. 65-83; 1404, pp. 84-109.

4. SAMA, Annual reports, 1404, p. 98.

5. *Middle East Economic Digest*, 12 July 1986, p. 22.

6. SAMA, *Annual reports*, 1401, p. 58; 1404, p. 74.

7. Ibid., p. 10.

8. SAMA, *Annual report*, 1404, p. 126.

9. *Financial Times*, 'Saudi Arabian Survey', 26 April 1982, p. 10.

10. Ibid.

11. *Middle East Economic Digest*, 5 July 1986, p. 24.

12. SAMA, *Annual report*, 1404, p. 87.

13. Industrial Studies and Development Center, *Guide to industrial investment in Saudi Arabia*, 4th edn, Riyadh, 1975, pp. 54-5.

14. SAMA, *Annual report*, 1404, p. 104.

8

Problems of the Financial Markets in the Gulf[1]

The growth of the financial markets in the Arabian Gulf has been very impressive since 1973, but those markets are now suffering from a number of ills which will have to be corrected to allow further progress. The main stumbling blocks appear to be the shortage of experienced personnel and the lack of a well-defined commercial law.

The personnel issue is perhaps the least problematic. Most of the banks and other financial institutions, until the late 1970s, had been staffed in majority by expatriate personnel. The top management was sometimes Saudi, Bahraini and Kuwaiti, but the middle management and a large number of the clerical staff were expatriate, either of other Arab countries or British and Indian. The institutions were prodded by the various governments and set up special training programs to Arabize the institutions. In Bahrain the banks started the Bahrain Bankers Training Center which trained staff in official as well as clerical skills. The center has been successful and is training hundreds of Bahrainis for positions in the local and international banks.

In Saudi the government started a similar training center. Today, in all the countries of the Gulf, as well as clerical positions, management is being entrusted more and more to local staff. The present slow down in the economy will accelerate the move towards complete management by local personnel as banks and other institutions start cutting costs and hence expensive expatriate personnel.

The main problem facing the financial industry in the Arab world, however, is the law. There has been little progress in the region on making the law adapt to the present-day economic situation. In fact, in Saudi Arabia, the legal developments have been mostly backwards.

In Bahrain and Kuwait, there is a commercial law which is mostly based on British traditions. In spite of the problems of the Souk Al Manakh, and the decline in petroleum revenues, the major defaults

and commercial disputes are being treated according to normal contractual law. In Saudi Arabia, however, there are no rules, no
jurisprudence — all decisions are left to the capricious interpretation
of Shari'a law by judges usually totally unfamiliar with the problems
and rules of modern trading. There is no part of the law which applies
to banks and borrowers.

Under King Faysal and the earlier years of King Khaled's reign,
the issue of legal difficulties for the financial institutions was mostly
unknown. The banks were allowed to register mortgages on fixed
assets, such as land and large buildings, although the legal counsels
did advise the banks against registering mortgages on moveable assets
as against the letter of the Holy Qur'an. Foreign banks were not
allowed to register mortgages but could use a local nominee to do
so, often a local friendly bank. In fact at least one American bank
was able to register a mortgage in its own name in 1977 in Jeddah.

The procedure for registration of mortgages was simple. The title
deed ('saq') was taken to the notary public, who would write on the
back of the deed that a certain amount had been borrowed by the owner
of the deed and that the property was mortgaged to the bank. The
mortgage was then also inscribed in the notary public registry. Mortgages were very common, banks securing many of their facilities in
this manner. SIDF in 1975 established some precedents on mortgages.
Since most factories were built on government-owned land, the borrowers could not just place mortgages on the land and 'what is on
it'. They had to establish a special title deed for the building itself
and 'what is in it', but excluding the land. Such a practice is common
in Europe and the US but had never been done before in Saudi. As
mentioned above, SIDF also managed to draft *pari passu* mortgages
with local banks to share the security on loans made by the two institutions to the same company. This procedure was very attractive to the
commercial banks, as they could feel secured in lending medium-term
funds, and be close and equal to the government-owned SIDF. The
borrower could also feel satisfied that he could finance his medium-
term needs with medium-term money from a variety of sources.

The mortgages, however, were not tested. Foreclosures by banks
were unknown. There had been reports that National Commercial
Bank foreclosed in the early 1970s on the warehouses of a merchant
in Jeddah, but it was not clear whether there were actual foreclosures,
or just an arrangement whereby the bank just received the title deeds
to the properties in settlement of its debt. Interest on the loans was
known to be 'haram', but both the banks and the borrowers seemed
satisfied to call 'riba' commissions and hope for the best. SAMA

itself did not lend locally with interest but did receive large amounts of 'riba' from the international banks and was very aggressive in obtaining the highest possible return on its money.

Naturally, in the booming economy of the 1970s, borrowers did not feel the burden of interest or even of loan repayments, and problems between banks and borrowers were minimal. In the recession of the following decade, however, conflicts became frequent, and exploitation of the weak legal system by the pressed borrowers became common.

The interpretation of the commercial law when applied to banks is fickle, and one has to refer to actual cases and judgements in the kingdom to discover what the law might be. The writer has compiled some real cases which have actually occurred in Saudi Arabia in the past five years, and which allow for some conclusions on the problems engendered by the present system.

I — A foreign bank was asked to make a loan to a Saudi company to be secured by a fleet of trench diggers and the guarantee of a prominent prince who owned the company through a nominee. The bank, aware that under the Shari'a law movable assets cannot be mortgaged, had checked with its own Saudi lawyer. The lawyer advised the bank that the security would be valid if a Saudi individual received possession of the equipment as trustee for the bank. The lawyer in a side agreement agreed to be trustee for the bank and act according to the bank's instructions. The lawyer received and registered a pledge from the borrower that the equipment belonged to him irrevocably. The lawyer also advised the bank that it should maximize its ability to obtain proper judgement and so should obtain a promissory note signed by the company and the prince as guarantor as well as a properly drafted guarantee from the prince. Eventually the company ran into difficulties and stopped payments on its debt. The bank then asked its lawyer to foreclose on the equipment. After some time, the lawyer informed the bank that repossession was impossible because the equipment had disappeared. It eventually showed up in a property belonging to the prince where the bank's lawyer felt it could not be repossessed.

The lawyer then advised the bank not to pursue its claim on equipment owned by the prince. It was also discovered that the equipment had already been financed once by a local distributor who eventually received the equipment back in settlement of his claim. The bank then called on the guarantee, to no avail. Eventually the bank took the case to court on the sole basis of the promissory note. For 18 months the bank tried to get a judgement, but never got past the hearings stage. The company was able to obtain delay after delay at the defendant's request. Some of the time the judges supposed to preside over the hearings would not show up. At any rate no progress was made.

To thicken the plot somewhat, it should be added that the loan had been made by the bank as part of an overall relationship with the prince. The bank had another facility with the prince's company, also guaranteed by the prince. The company, a small contractor, had obtained from the bank a performance bond and an advance payment guarantee issued in favor of a major contractor for the subcontracting, of large road works. This main contractor had himself, obtained the contract from the government by bidding for the job at what he knew would probably be a loss. The main contractor was hoping to make up some of the losses by subcontracting, at a great gain to himself, most of the job to a small unsophisticated subcontractor like the prince's company which would eventually have to finish the work, at whatever cost, in order to protect the name of its principal. The small subcontractor being offered the first large contract of their existence were swayed by the large figures and convinced that it could do the job at a profit. Further the main contractor felt comforted by the PB and APG issued by the bank, knowing that it could call on it at any time. In fact one could suspect that the main contractor planned all along to get the work done by the prince and also call the bonds.

The bank, being aware of the reputation of the main contractor, and knowing the problems of dealing with a prominent member of the royal family, secured itself by taking 50 per cent cash collateral on the PB and the APG, and drafted the guarantees according to the SAMA text but with a few conditions and a time limit. The prince's company was not able to perform under the subcontract, and the main contractor called the bonds. Unfortunately for him the conditions which the bank had placed in the bonds were not met, and the bank refused to pay. At the same time the bank could not obtain payment from the prince under his guarantee of the facility secured by the trench diggers and the court case in Riyadh did not move. The bank then cancelled the PB and APG, took the cash collateral and changed it into a deposit from the prince and set off (netted out) the loan from the deposit.

Naturally, these actions from all the parties gave rise to lawsuits. The bank sued the prince in Riyadh for non-payment under the guarantee, the main contractor threatened to sue the bank, but himself being in partial liquidation could not follow up his threat. The amount of the deposit used to set off the loan was larger than the loan, and therefore the prince was very upset, claiming that the bank had stolen his money. Poorly advised by his managers, the prince sued the bank in Bahrain to recover the deposit through his company. This suit was favorable to the bank, because it meant that the prince's company accepted the jurisdiction of Bahrain. Immediately the bank counter-sued the company for lack of payment on the trench diggers loan, and asked the court to mix the suits, as well as officially cancel the bonds issued for the company in favor of the main contractor. Eventually, the prince discovered he could not influence the Bahraini court, and withdrew his suit before judgment, leaving the whole matter pending, and for all intents and purposes settled in favor of the bank.

It appears from the above saga that the legal system in Saudi when it comes to banks should be read as follows:

1. Efforts to create new legal precedents will fail. Such effort is commendable but obviously difficult, and not part of the legal tradition.

2. All the documentation supporting the loan, the facility letter, the pledge and possession of the movable assets was useless and not even reviewed in court. Only the promissory note and guarantee were accepted instruments, and even then were not enough to ensure recovery.

3. One of the main factors in the above process was the bank's opposition to a party above the law. Hence, whatever the security may be and however tight the documentation, there is a definite 'fait du prince' problem.

4. The Bahraini court had a more professional approach to the problems, and apparently did not include religious matters in its review of the case. Of course the court in Bahrain was not under a 'fait du prince' pressure, and could have been trusted to provide a fair review and judgment.

II — In another example, a small merchant gave a foreign bank a promissory note and post-dated checks drawn on a Saudi bank in support of a guarantee in favor of a second Saudi bank, which in turn made a cash advance to the small merchant. At maturity of the loan the Saudi bank was not repaid, and the guarantee of the foreign bank was called and paid. The foreign bank presented the post-dated checks at maturity for payment to cover the disbursement it had to make to the Saudi bank under the guarantee. By then, there were no funds to back the checks, which were returned. The foreign bank gave the checks to its lawyer for enforcement. Theoretically, the procedure for bounced checks is very rapid and brings about immediate imprisonment of the guilty party. In this case, however, the debtor in spite of the regulations drafted by the council of ministers on bounced checks, stated that the bank did not really have a claim on him. The case was sent to a civil court where the bank had to prove its claim. Eventually the bank managed to get an order from a judge calling for the arrest of the man. After many weeks of delays from the police, the man was duly picked up and released two hours later. The bank was never repaid.

The lessons here are:

1. Enforcement of post-dated checks by banks is at best ineffective.

2. More important, enforcement of court decisions in non-criminal matters is not automatic. The police will reserve the right to decide whether a decision is worth enforcing depending on their own review of the case.

III — A contractor who had obtained a contract from a government agency failed to perform and, as sometimes happens in extreme cases, the advance payment guarantee was called by the agency. The agency, however, called the guarantee after its expiry date. Hence, in good faith the bank refused to pay. The agency took the case to court and won on the grounds, one can presume, that the guarantee had not been returned and that the intention having been to pay should the bond be called, this intention should remain valid whatever the time elapsed may be. In other words, the court decided that the account party and the beneficiary could modify the instrument without recourse by the bank.

This judgment, which took place in 1982, has been disturbing to the banks. The SAMA text of guarantees which is used under most contracts is totally unconditional and on call; the bank's only protection against abusive calls is the expiry date. Fortunately there are no examples of abusive calls by any of the ministries and few of substance from agencies. However the temptation to abuse is great. In this case one can suspect that the agency of the government simply forgot to ask for an extension or a renewal of the guarantee prior to their maturity. To avoid penalties the civil servants in charge of managing construction of projects for the agency probably took the case to court to intimidate the bank into renewing the facilities. Whatever the cause, the consequence can be far reaching, because it implies that the

Saudi courts cannot be trusted to apply the normal international practices on documentary credits. On the less negative side, however, the bank could have taken heart in the fact that another court in Saudi may just as well have decided in favor of the bank.

IV — In the same area of documentary credits, there has been an unconfirmed rumor that a bank has lost a court battle against a merchant who had refused to pay the bank back on a letter of credit. Apparently the bank had opened a letter of credit for a Saudi importer. The advising bank in the exporter's country had negotiated the document and been paid by the opening bank. The goods were received in the kingdom and delivered to the importer. The opening bank was out of pocket, put the importer's account in overdraft and asked him to reimburse the bank. The importer then claimed that the goods were defective and simply refused to pay the bank. In due course, the bank sued the importer because according to the Uniform Commercial Code regulations which regulate international trade world-wide, the banks are only responsible for the consistency of the documents, and not for the actual goods. This point is important, because the banks could not possibly check the goods ex-factory, on board and at delivery. Should they be made responsible for such checking the actual volume of international trade would greatly suffer. The problems of defective goods are to be handled between the buyer and the seller directly. Normally the seller would sue the buyer in his own country and try to obtain enforcement of the judgment against the seller. In this case the bank sued the buyer and lost, as the court made the bank responsible to ensure that the goods were not defective. Should this rumor prove true it would show that once again a Saudi court made a judgment or is rumored to have made a judgment going against all the international precedents.

In all these cases it seems clear that in financial disputes involving banks there is no jurisprudence. A court in Riyadh may decide one way on a case while a court in Dammam decides differently on a similar case, or even the same court may decide differently at different times.

The banks in the Gulf have tried to cope with the potential problems of court bias against them by using various techniques, such as:

1. Using promissory notes which show no interest, for example a $10 million promissory note for a $9 million loan discounted up front; or two sets of notes, one for capital and one for interest. Banks also have called interest and fees 'commissions'. Such semantics

have proven useless as the opponent can (and does) simply point them out to the judge, who rules them to be interest and nets them out of the debt.

2. Banks have been known to use a Saudi agent, usually a lawyer, to register assets to be used as security in his name on their behalf. For instance, since mortgages taken by banks are not acceptable to the courts, the borrower can agree to sell his land for a nominal price to the bank's agent, with a buy-back clause at termination of the banking facility. The title deed is then registered in the agent's name. At the same time, the bank signs a trusteeship agreement with its agent which covers the bank, and whereby the agent agrees irrevocably to follow all the bank's instructions, with regard to the property 'owned' by the agent. The borrower signs a letter giving the trustee the right to arrange the sale of the security on first demand.

There are two problems with this approach: (A) The agent must be 100 per cent reliable. It is not unheard of to find that if the bank wants to foreclose on the security, the agent starts showing signs of unhappiness and suggests to the bank that a more equitable share of the proceeds should be given to him. (B) The seller is always unhappy if the security is sold and will usually threaten to sue the bank and the agent on the grounds that the price obtained is too low.

In both cases the bank is in a strong position if covered by a good trustee agreement; nevertheless, it can be a most frustrating situation and the bank is never sure that the judges will not question the intent of the bank as wilful infringement of the law.

3. Banks in Wall Street fashion will draw up long blanket loan agreements covering what seem to be all the potential problems. It appears however, that the longer the agreement the less likely it is that it will be read by the court. Hence in cases of litigation they are useless. On the other hand they have the advantage of satisfying head offices and legal counsels not quite aware of Saudi practices. Long agreements can also be of use when the banks feel that they can pursue a customer in Europe or the US. If no legal action is planned or feasible outside the kingdom, simple documents of four or five pages in Arabic describing the transaction and showing repayment dates with a set-off and default clause seem to suffice.

Most Eurodollar agreements ask for legal opinions stating that the borrower has the right to borrow and that the law applicable to the agreement is valid and enforceable. Of course in Saudi Arabia lawyers cannot vouch for the last part of the normal opinion, but opinions have been asked and given with proper warnings on the lack of jurisprudence, and loans made in spite of the warnings.

In sum, it appears that none of the legal loopholes will work in the Saudi courts. In case of trouble, the bankers are left only with private negotiations with the defaulter emphasizing reputation, family, duties, and the like, and constant visits to wear down the stone until one of the parties settles out of sheer fatigue. Because of these difficulties, the bank must take great care in evaluating each credit arrangement and obtain a great deal of information on the reputation of each potential client. Foreign banks, furthermore, should limit their efforts to certain products. They should avoid:

— All medium-term loans. This is to avoid greater losses on interest, by-pass downturns in the economy, sudden changes in regulations, and so on.

— All facilities that need security to look attractive and safe unless, of course, the security is held outside the kingdom.

— All facilities more or less subject to 'fait du prince'.

Most banks have emphasized the less risky business of trade finance, letters of credit, bonds, refinancing and the like. This business itself is not without pitfalls as the banks have no lien on goods once landed, but at least there is a potential cash flow from the sales, which, from a credit standpoint, is desirable, even if legally the bank has no easy way to get hold of it. Of course for most banks the bread and butter has been the issuance of bid and performance bonds, as well as the advance payment guarantees for contractors, and on the whole this has been a very satisfactory business because of the government's extreme caution in calling the bonds and guarantees.

The government ministries have always acted in good faith and never abused their right to call the guarantees and bonds. In fact, in the case of Saudi companies, the ministries have even gone to great lengths to ease the problems of troubled contractors and hence of the banks. The only common problem has been in the assignment of payments. Normally a bank issuing performance bonds, advance payment guarantees and other facilities related to a given project will demand that payments made to the contractor be directed to the account of the bank, which in turn can keep some of the money to reduce any outstanding debt and disburse the balance to the contractor for his direct expenses. The normal procedure is for the contractor to give an irrevocable letter to his client, asking that all payments be made to the contractor's account in the Saudi bank. The bank asks that the client acknowledges the letter, which is often not done. Finally, the contractor gives the right to banks to block all the payments received by the bank from the client. A normal assignment can be subject to many loopholes and a number of contractors have managed to get hold first of funds normally bound for the bank's assignment account. This usually happens at the local bank level and usually through clerical errors, but it can make the assignment a doubtful security.

In Bahrain today, all banks are aware of the potential legal problems related to loans in Saudi Arabia and as a consequence have decided to greatly limit their involvement in commercial banking and move into investment banking. The switch in business line is probably pleasing to SAMA which will see a decline in foreign bank influence in the kingdom, and hence increase its hold over the local economy.

The move to investment banking in the Gulf may not be easy. The various products which make investment banking take a great deal of expertise and experience. Portfolio management and sale of securities has long been a Swiss speciality in the Gulf. The Swiss banks have an image of professionalism which takes many years to build, and which very few of the banks established in the Gulf have. Banks and financial institutions are also trying to get into sales of shares, mergers and acquisitions. Whatever the investment banking product may be, one can expect sooner or later a transfer of funds to the bank exchanged for an asset by the local Arab investors. Until now the foreign banks specializing in this type of product have been very successful, although very discreet. However if all the banks in the region start peddling their investment banking wares, there may be some annoyance from the Saudi and other authorities that banks are trying to take funds out of the local economy. Should this concern arise the Saudi government could try to limit the foreign banks' access to the customers in the kingdom.

There is a section of the commercial code which says:

ARTICLE 5 — No person without fixed premises for carrying on his occupation may act as importer, exporter, contractor, broker, commission agent, agent or commercial intermediary unless he obtains a license to do so from the Register of Commerce Bureau situated in the area where his residence or place of activity is located in the Kingdom . . .

(Law no. 54 dated 29.4.1375 H)

Should the relevant authorities ever feel the transfers of funds ought to be limited, this paragraph leaves the door open for restriction of the investment activities by foreign banks. Article 5 of the code has been invoked once (in 1983) against unscrupulous persons trying to sell foreign assets which were not as *bona fide* as they claimed. These persons were expelled from the kingdom. Some of the large international banks had representatives living in the kingdom and selling investment services for a number of years. These offices, though under the sponsorship of well known Saudis, were asked to close, but the same banks are still able to send officers to Saudi Arabia regularly using visitors' visas.

Until 1986 SAMA has not attempted to intervene or help the banks caught in legal wrangles. In May 1986, however, it advised the banks to include in their loan agreements language which would emphasize the contractual relationship between the bank and the borrower.[2] At the same time the ministry of commerce 'has empowered its legal committee to hear disputes between banks and their customers'.[3] So far, however, this approach has not been tested in court, and from the past experiences it seems that the advice from SAMA and the involvement of the legal committee of the ministry of commerce will not bring much success, as any borrower will have the right to take his case to the Shari'a court. Rightly or wrongly, banks feel the Shari'a judges see them as 'creatures of the devil', which entice the unwary to sin. Hence, equitable judgments do not seem any closer.

In 1986 some of the large merchants, with large loans from the foreign banks have taken advantage of the legal situation in Saudi Arabia *vis-à-vis* the banks. The merchants, knowing very well that the foreign banks are powerless in the kingdom, have defaulted on their debts and are negotiating with the banks from a position of strength on the writing down of portions of the loans and rescheduling of maturities. Unfortunately, the defaults of the few will hurt the whole economy. With declining revenues the government is counting on the private sector to pick the investments which it will not be able to make to continue the industrialization of the kingdom. In turn, the private sector will have to rely on banks, insurance companies, et al. to provide medium-term financing to build factories. Unfortunately, the banks are fully aware that the safety of their money is at the mercy of the borrower, without any chance for fair arbitration in the courts. Consequently, the already meager flow of medium-term funds for private borrowers, which had mostly come from foreign banks, has dwindled to almost nothing. It is unlikely that large banks, both Saudi and foreign, will again lend to the Saudi mechants and industrialists until a major change in the law takes place.

The solutions to the legal problems in Saudi must come soon or else the economy and the development of the kingdom will be strangled. Reforming the legal structure, however, will demand political decisions which must remove the Shari'a court involvement in economic disputes, or reform the Shari'a courts so that there will be judges with enough knowledge of business and economics to understand the disputes presented to them; an introduction of a system of jurisprudence, at least in terms of economic disputes, is also needed.

The Saudi legal system is of prime importance to the other countries in the Gulf. Saudi is the largest, richest and most powerful of the countries in the region; hence, if because of its inability to provide a fair and stable commercial law it is likely to halt the industrialization of the kingdom, the chances are that the surrounding countries will be affected as well. Among others, the Bahraini economy, which is dependent on servicing the wealth of its neighbor, will suffer from a decline in banking business from the OBUs, which in turn could affect the political stability of the country and hence of the whole region.

NOTES

1. Substantial parts of this chapter were published by the author in *Middle East Executive Reports*, March 1985, vol. 8, no. 9.

2. *Middle East Economic Digest*, 20 May 1986, p. 19.

3. Ibid., p. 20.

9

The Future of the Markets

As of 1986, the Arabian Gulf is facing one of the most difficult times it has seen in the twentieth century. The war between Iran and Iraq is exacerbating some of the internal social problems between religious sects. It is a drain on the resources of the nations as they finance part of the Iraqi war effort. It also indirectly contributes to the decline in oil prices. Indeed, if production by Iran and Iraq is much lower than before the war started, both countries are presently under great pressure to sell whatever they can produce at whatever price, just to raise cash. Deep discounting by Iran and Iraq affects the market as a whole and puts downward pressure on all producers. Ironically, peace, whenever it happens, will have the same effect, as production capacity of both countries will rise dramatically and their needs for rebuilding the economies will be staggering.

The world-wide decline in oil prices has left the Gulf nations with good cash reserves but an economy not yet adapted to more conservative, and even negative, balance of payments. The vast amounts of government money are no longer available to subsidize the population. The local industries which have been started are not yet able to compete in world markets, and will greatly depend on protectionist policies to survive, which by themselves will bring increases in prices and decreases in quality for the local consumers, thereby bringing a decline in overall standards of living.

In Kuwait the cost of the Souk Al Manakh has weakened the financial system to the point where it is entirely reliant on the government, which in turn has had to dig deeply in its reserves, just at a time when income has become scarce.

In the previous chapter we discussed the problems of the law in the region. Certainly if the law is not adapted to allow for proper and just commercial arbitration, the markets will not be able to meet the challenges of the future. One of the most hopeful aspects of the developments of the past five years in the Gulf has been the very quiet but steady progress made by the Gulf Cooperation Council (GCC). This EEC-type arrangement has been working slowly but surely to harmonize policies and economies. The problems of commercial law have not yet been solved in the context of the GCC. However, the council does provide a good forum for overall commercial disputes to be reviewed in a manner satisfactory to all. One can hope that a commercial court will be established by the GCC, with enough power to implement its decisions in all the countries, leaving the local Shari'a courts with small commercial disputes and criminal law. Should the governments of the GCC not be able to curb the unprofessional judicial reviews of the Saudi courts with regard to commercial disputes, the financial markets will not be able to develop further and help the economies adapt to the present problems. The Deputy Secretary of the GCC, Abdel Aziz Al Qwaiz, in a speech to the Arab Bankers Association of North America on 1 May 1986, hinted that the GCC was aware of the legal problems and suggested it was developing inter-GCC laws to cope with the problems.[1]

The banks in Bahrain have recognized that they cannot continue solely providing loans and letters of credit for Saudi customers. The legal problems discussed earlier, as well as the lower spreads on facilities, and in general difficult loans to Latin America, Africa, and the Middle East, are deterring the American and European banks from their traditional commercial banking activities. Most commercial banks are attempting to develop the types of business which, until recently, had been largely the domain of investment and merchant banks, such as mergers and acquisitions, securities trading, and advisory services. However, changing from commercial banking to investment banking is not easy. The products which can be offered by the Bahrain-based banks require a great deal of credibility and trust by the customers. Thus, although investment banking does produce large fee income with less risk than conventional banking, the establishment of such capacity takes a long time to develop.

The major fee earners for investment banks are mergers and acquisitions. In Bahrain the banks can offer such services to local firms trying to acquire firms in the Western world and in the Arabian peninsula. Being the intermediary on an acquisition takes great skill, and the banks are competing with the long- and well-established European and American investment houses. Over time the banks may develop enough knowledge in the various markets to play such a role. The branches of certain foreign banks in Bahrain have already played this role in finding proper real estate and industrial investments for high net worth individuals. The major part of the work has been done in the home offices, but the contact point has been the local branch. In reverse the banks based in the Arabian Gulf can develop their customer base in the area and let their branches overseas find the investments and manage the negotiations. One of the local institutions, Investcorp, has been so far quite successful in arranging leverage buy-outs of companies in the United States. Investcorp, with a small capital of US$ 50 million, is considered in the Gulf as the trail blazer for all Arab institutions. Investcorp has only worked outside the region and not yet used its merchant banking skills to merge or acquire local firms.

The development of mergers and acquisitions within the Arabian Gulf is hindered again by the laws and the traditions. There are only very few publicly-held companies, and most of them are controlled by the governments. Hence the buying of shares on the markets to obtain control is not feasible. The main vehicle for corporate investments is through limited liability companies, which are subject to approval by all shareholders for any change in ownership. However, the GCC has agreed to eventually allow all the citizens of the member states to purchase shares and assets in each other's states. The rule is not yet fully enforced, but today some Kuwaiti citizens own land in Bahrain, and some Bahrainis have interests in Saudi companies. Hence, in the near future, one can see that the banks, especially the Bahraini ones, will have a role to play as intermediaries between firms and investors. The banks will have to be aggressive in trying (1) to get mandates from potential sellers and (2) approach potential buyers, and *vice versa*. They will need to build their pool of information and build their human resources to go after this type of business. All of which will take years to build.

The issuance of commercial paper and the floating of shares for private companies is also a potential business available to banks, especially in a market where the banks are becoming more conservative. Freely exchangeable paper has never yet been issued in the markets in the Gulf, and there is no secondary market for it at this time. Again, in the near future, the very stable and large industrial concerns may go to the market, if led by a reputable and stable bank such as GIB or National Bank of Kuwait, and float paper which eventually could be held by other firms or even individuals, as investment instruments. Such a development would be a major boost for the financial markets, as it would create work for the banks and the need for a market place to trade the instruments. Perhaps it should be suggested that the government of the GCC 'seeds' the markets by providing freely transferable commercial paper issued by a GCC government-owned corporation such as ASRY or ALBA, or even GIB.

In early 1986, Al Bank Al Saudi Al Fransi in Saudi Arabia tried to issue a RUF (Revolving Underwriting Facility) for two customers. These facilities are commitments by the banks to lend short-term money on a revolving basis at the request of the borrower. The borrower has the option to borrow or not to borrow at his convenience and pays a commitment fee for the service. The issues were great successes, but SAMA has vetoed any further such issuance. SAMA's role in this case has been somewhat puzzling. The RUFs are relatively new instruments in the markets in Europe, and SAMA was probably worried that the firms borrowing the funds would only do so when they would be least expected to repay, hence endangering the banks. On the other hand, these instruments have been popular with the banks because of the commitment fee paid on an unfunded risk, which improves the average return on assets of the banks — a very tempting proposition in a declining market. In spite of SAMA's negative approach, one can foresee that more and more such issues will be made in the markets, either through the local banks or through the Bahraini entities.

The banks can also develop more portfolio management business. This product is attractive to the banks as they make fees on the purchase and sale of instruments for customers. Until now, portfolio management was done mainly by the Swiss banks, with some German, English and American banks arranging investment in their respective local currencies and instruments. Lately the Investment Banking License banks in Bahrain (IBLs), mostly the Japanese-owned ones, have developed large and successful sales efforts of Japanese securities, bringing some depth to the market. The stranglehold of the Swiss banks on portfolio management is rapidly decreasing and the role of the local banks should increase.

A number of banks organized real estate funds for investments in Europe or in the United States, currency funds, etc. Most of these funds, however were unsuccessful, usually because they were floated by banks or investment companies that did not have the recognition necessary to make the investors feel comfortable with the management of the funds, and because they came to the market before customers were familiar with these instruments. The issuance of certificates in various investment funds, somewhat akin to mutual funds in the Western countries, will most likely develop. However to be successful the issuers will have to be well known and accepted in the region. Further, they will have to maintain a sales force to sell the instruments to private individuals and institutions. They will also have to convince the potential buyers that the instruments are very liquid and can be sold easily at a minimum loss, at any time. In 1986 the Gulf International Bank started issuing certificates of investments, called Unit Trusts, for which it publishes a value weekly. Similar certificates are issued by banks in Saudi Arabia. The Unit Trusts are a mix of mutual funds and certificates of deposit. GIB uses the funds it has gathered from its customers to invest in various market instruments and manages the portfolio in a professional manner, taking advantage of its size to maximize profits. The amount portfolio is divided in small pieces, the Unit Trusts, the value of which is given weekly and includes the gains or losses made on the portfolio. The advantage to the customer is that it can always sell the Unit Trust back to the bank at the bid value published weekly. The bank is also a large gainer in this product because it obtains deposits, and makes profits on the management of the portfolio. Perhaps in the future such Unit Trusts could be issued and saleable not only back to the issuing bank but to the public at large. This would give rise to a larger market, which would develop liquidity among investors, and encourage capital markets. It may be too early to tell of the success of these new instruments, but should they be successful they would indicate a major shift in the public acceptance of modern financial instruments.

The American banks in Bahrain, like most other banks, have been moving away from commercial banking and have been developing personal banking and portfolio management, competing with the Swiss Banks. Arab banks and money changers under the leadership of Arab Banking Corporation (ABC) have started to develop their own Visa traveller's checks denominated in dollars and even in Saudi riyals.

The Gulf banks have also started to expand and diversify beyond the Arabian region. Most banks have opened branches in New York, London and Singapore, but have also started to acquire institutions. ABC has bought 70 per cent of Banco Atlantico in Spain and Sung Hung Kai Bank in Hong Kong, and Kuwait Asia has opened a merchant bank in Australia.[2]

There are numbers of other investment instruments which can be developed in the Arabian Gulf in the near future. For instance, as was seen earlier, insurance companies, which play only a minimal role at this time, could start developing the syndication of risks to private individuals, somewhat like the Lloyd's syndications. They could also start investing the premiums earned in at least some of the local instruments now offered by the local banks, and in general take more of a part in the local financial markets. *MEED*, in its special report on Saudi Arabia of May 1986, said that the Gulf Cooperation Council may create a large intra-GCC reinsurance company. This development would come at a time when the General Insurance Company of Saudi (the equivalent to Social Security in the United States) has invested SR 500 million in a new insurance venture in the kingdom, to be run according to 'Islamic principles'.[3]

The stock markets will also have a role to play. The situation of equity-financing at present is reeling from the effects of the Souk Al Manakh, and probably at this time no one will try to float shares in any ventures however worthy. However, as the industrialization of the region proceeds, there is a great need for private investment. A fresh development of the stock market could be achieved if the governments of the GCC acted in common to promote common regulations and controls throughout the countries of the council so that share dealings could be made between all the countries of the Gulf. Companies by shares should be allowed to be established without the difficulty of having royal decrees in Saudi Arabia. On the other hand all firms wishing to float shares in the markets should provide proper audited statements and extensive disclosure of activities such as a 10K report in the US to all potential investors. The markets should be open so that all know what activity takes place in which stock, a ticker-tape type of information. As has been done in Kuwait, the companies exchanged on the trading floor must be approved and monitored by a professional group. Finally, and again following the Kuwait example of early 1986, shares of foreign companies should be traded on the local exchange. This will give the average investor the habit of investing in relatively secured shares, which can then be extended to good local companies.

Perhaps, however, one could go further. The establishment of a Gulf stock exchange has been suggested by a number of people (among whom, Ebrahim Eshaq Abdul Rahman, the Managing Director of Bank of Bahrain and Kuwait[4]) which ideally should be placed in Bahrain, as the most advanced international financial center in the region. The development of an intra-Gulf stock market in Bahrain would help develop the private investments in the Gulf. However, an intra Gulf market, if limited to the GCC citizens, will remain small and regional. The present successes of the stock markets of New York and London are not only due to the high quality of their regulatory institutions. They are also active because they are open to all citizens of all countries, not only to EEC or American citizens. Today foreigners can invest in the region, but the procedure is long, complicated, and the tax implications very unfavorable. It is the opinion of the writer that the markets in the Gulf are overly parochial. In the long run it makes the whole region very sensitive to swings in oil prices which are exacerbated by flights of capital. The Gulf Arabs have the right to buy and sell real estate, shares, and securities freely in Western Europe and the United States, and indeed have used this right extensively. By limiting investments in their own region to local persons, the Gulf Arab states are limiting not only money flows into the region, but the development of ideas and talent. They are certainly protecting their sovereignty, but they are also promoting their own isolation. Freedom of investment would not bring about a flurry of take-overs by foreign entities such as the large multi-nationals. The large international firms are too wary of the political risks inherent to the region, but it could help the development of small industries, which, if numerous, are the real basis for development.

NOTES

1. Arab Bankers National Association, *Newsletter*, vol. III, no. 2, June 1986.
2. *Arab Banking and Finance*, April 1985, p. 6.
3. *Middle East Economic Digest*, 15 November 1986, p. 14.
4. *Arab banking and finance handbook*, 1985, p. 117.

Conclusion

The financial markets of the three nations of the Arabian Gulf which we have studied are controlled by Sunni beduin families which are relatively close cousins. The fact that the different governments have fashioned the financial markets of their countries differently shows that, in spite of the similarity in leadership, they had to adapt to the different needs and aspirations of their people.

In Saudi Arabia, King Fahad, since he came to the throne, and perhaps even more so as adviser to King Faysal and King Khaled, led the move of the kingdom towards heavy industrialization. The King may have felt that the consolidation of the power of the Saud family and the unification of the kingdom could only be assured by changing society from a mosaic of tribes owing allegiance to their own leaders to a modern and unified population looking to the central government for guidance. To have the population feel they could transfer their allegiance from tribe to nation and from sheikh to King, it was important to have all citizens perceive the King as the source of their wealth and income. To achieve the ability to bestow wealth to its citizens the King had to develop the economy of the country. Development had to account for Saudi Arabia's characteristics which are cheap energy, large capital, and low population. These three parameters implied that any economic growth would have to be based on a modern and widespread industrialization, rich in technology. The financial markets were thus built to promote these industrial policies, while ensuring that all loans, licenses, subsidies and hence profits had to be seen as emanating from the government.

Through the ministry of finance, and the ministry's control over the monetary agency, the King slowly but surely came to control all the financial institutions. First the foreign banks were Saudi-ized, and, little by little, the influence of SAMA on their management is being felt. The Islamic banks were not allowed to develop in the kingdom, although, logically, the kingdom should have been their cradle. The money changers still have a relative amount of independence but are increasingly under pressure to come under the control of SAMA. The activities of the foreign banks, whether Arab or not and whether operating in the kingdom or from Bahrain, have been very substantially curbed. The present recession, in a backhanded manner, is helping SAMA curb the institutions it does not yet control. The problems in the region such as the Iran-Iraq war, which precipitated the stock market crash, allowed SAMA and the ministry of finance to abort any liberalization of the shares market in Saudi, which could have been difficult to control, as a successful stock exchange could develop into a successful source of capital independent from government largesse.

On a less political level it must be said that SAMA's efforts have certainly stabilized the financial system. They have helped maintain a high level of trust in the banks, and in general protected the public. On the other hand SAMA and the ministries of finance, of commerce and of industry have not been willing or able to tackle the promotion of a modernization of the commercial code with good and binding commercial legal courts. Some of the large Saudi borrowers, under pressure because of decreased activity in the region, used the subordination of the commercial code to the Shari'a law to avoid repayments due to banks, hence creating a sudden self-restraint on the part of the foreign banks which until then were active in the kingdom. The Saudi banks themselves are unwilling to place their funds in the private economy, stifling somewhat the development of the kingdom. The banks are very liquid and, besides short-term trade type financing, either place their riyals in other banks or at SAMA, or finance the large government-controlled companies such as SABIC, Petromin or Saudia. The goal of modern industrialization in the kingdom will remain hampered by the lack of proper commercial law. An imposition by the King of the changes needed would certainly upset a large segment of the conservative population, who may not be happy with the development process in the first place. Another factor which will delay development is the self-limitation created by the over-centralization of the economic policy. The government has mapped the industrialization, and no private industry will succeed if it does not fit in the mold, as it would have to start without the benefits of cheap land on industrial estates, SIDF, and may not even get the licenses required. It would add greater depth to the economy to encourage small industry and in general venture capital projects presented by the young but not wealthy.

In Kuwait the very liberal policy of the government has brought about a situation somewhat similar to that of Saudi. The laissez-faire attitude encouraged a runaway speculation on shares and real estate fuelled by the large amounts of cash which found their way from the government to the public. The subsequent crash in both the share and the real estate markets forced the intervention of the government, which limited the fall of the markets and the impact on the citizens by massive purchases of shares.

Kuwait was the most sophisticated financial center in the Middle

East. The Kuwaiti investment companies were very active in investment banking before the concept dawned on most banks in Saudi and in Bahrain. They created instruments in local currencies, they were very active in the European markets as syndication managers on loans, bonds and floating rate notes in all the major currencies of the world. Kuwait was also very active in the world stock markets, buying shares for investment for the future generations of Kuwait.

It appears that Kuwait, having decided that it is small but rich, with a relatively more homogeneous population than Saudi Arabia or Bahrain, could become the center of a kind of holding company for investments abroad. The profits from these investments could bring good income to the population and shift the wealth from oil to financial holdings. The local development of commerce and industry was left to happen on its own, except for the transfers from the government to its citizens in the form of land purchases and support of the stock markets. Those transfers to the population are in great part what encouraged runaway speculation and caused the crisis of 1982, forcing the government to intervene very strongly in the private economy, and thus come to control the economy as tightly as in Saudi Arabia. It is hoped that when peace finally comes to the region and later when prices of petroleum start rising again, that the Kuwaiti government will emphasize a lightly controlled freedom of investment, and avoid the transfers that fuelled the speculation.

For its part the Bahraini government was able to review its strengths and weaknesses, and, without the use of heavy-handed planning, mapped out its own strategy for the future. Having declining oil resources, very small cash reserves, and a small but very diversified and educated population, Bahrain decided to develop a service economy. Bahrain adapted its laws so that both the Gulf firms as well as the foreign firms were able to get established. The financial institutions in need of a place in the Middle East after the death of Beirut chose Bahrain to establish their commercial banks, investment banks, offshore servicing companies, leasing companies etc. Bahrain remained open for the establishment of Islamic banks, and insurance companies. Until mid-1986 the main financial market activity missing in Bahrain is that of a stock exchange. The crash of the Souk Al Manakh in Kuwait put a damper on the Bahraini plans to become the stock market of the region.

Bahrain is in a prime position to take advantage of the developments which are taking place in the region because of the Gulf Cooperation Council. The Bahraini government's economic and trade policies, which are characterized by benevolent controls, will keep Bahrain as the financial center of the region. It is hoped that a GCC stock exchange will develop in Bahrain, as it will deepen the existing market and diversify away from banking.

Political stability is the main purpose of the GCC, and the factor that forces the governments to make the necessary efforts towards an increasing unification of their countries. The economic unification, which is the least difficult of the issues, will profit the state of Bahrain the most. In spite of its small size Bahrain has a strategic value to the GCC and its population must be kept relatively happy. Further, it is, with Kuwait, the most open to modern systems of management for financial markets.

With declining revenues, and bled by the Iran-Iraq conflict, the Gulf nations face a very challenging future. Not least among the concerns is that the next generation of leaders will have to maintain the existing welfare and cater to the aspirations of the populations. Hopefully the Gulf leadership will further develop the existing financial markets to offset the present difficulties in the region.

Bibliography

BOOKS AND ARTICLES

Abdel Rahman and Ibrahim Eshaq, 'Gulf stockmarkets: change of attitude is necessary', article in *Arab banking and finance handbook*, Falcon, Bahrain, 1985.

Ahmad, Ziauddin, 'The present state of the Islamic finance movement', in *The impact and role of Islamic banking in international finance: issues and prospects*, a conference of the US Arab Chamber of Commerce, 28 June 1985, New York.

Arab Banking Corporation, *The Arab economies, structure and outlook*, Bahrain, 1983.

Arabian American Oil Company, Public Relations Department, *Facts and figures*, Dharan, Saudi Arabia, 1984.

Asa'ad, Yunis, *The legal and practical guide to doing business in Kuwait*, 3 vols, Kuwait, 1979.

Attia, Gamal El-Din, 'The origins and foundations of Islamic banking and financial principles', in *The impact and role of Islamic banking in international finance: issues and prospects*, a conference of the US Arab Chamber of Commerce, 28 June 1985, New York.

Bahrain Monetary Agency, *Quarterly Bulletin*.

El-Beblaoui, Hazem, *The Arab Gulf economy in a turbulent age*, Croom Helm, London, 1984.

Bindagi, Hussein Hamza, *Atlas of Saudi Arabia*, Oxford University Press, Oxford, 1978.

Chase World Information Corporation, *Developing business in the Middle East and North Africa:Saudi Arabia*.

Chase World Information Corporation, *Agribusiness potential in the Middle East and North Africa: Saudi Arabia*.

Central Bank of Kuwait, *Annual report*, no. 16, Kuwait,1984/5.

Central Bank of Kuwait, *Economic chart book*, vol. 7, Kuwait, 1985.

El Darwish, Ahmed Sani, 'Islamic financial principles: an overview of opportunities and issues', in *The impact and role of Islamic banking in international finance: issues and prospects*, a conference of the US Arab Chamber of Commerce, 28 June 1985, New York.

Fougerouse, Maurice, *Bahrein. L'instant perdu*, Paris, 1983.

Homood, S.H., *Islamic banking*, Arab Information, London, 1985.

Homood, S.H., 'Islamic banking: limited knowledge restrains progress', article in *Arab banking and finance handbook*, Falcon, Bahrain, 1985.

Homood, S.H. 'Islamic banking and social development', in *The impact and role of Islamic banking in international finance: issues and prospects*, a conference of the US Arab Chamber of Commerce, 28 June 1985, New York.

International Monetary Fund, *Survey of Arab banks*, 8 February 1982.

International Monetary Fund, *International financial statistics*, February 1986.

Industrial Studies and Development Center, *Guide to industrial investment in Saudi Arabia*, 4th edn, Riyadh, 1974

Kubursi, A.A., *Oil, industrialization & development in the Arab Gulf states*, Croom Helm, London, 1984.

Al Mallakh, Ragaie and Dorothea, *Saudi Arabia, energy developmental planning and industrialization*, Lexington Books, Lexington, Mass., 1982.

Moore, Alan, 'Bahrain's offshore banking units', article in *Arab banking and finance handbook*, Falcon, Bahrain, 1983.

Nakhjavani, Mehran, 'Plus ça change . . . Kuwait crash of '82', article in *Arab banking and finance handbook*, Falcon, Bahrain, 1983.

Nakhjavani, Mehran, *Arab banks and the international financial markets*, MEPEP, Nicosia, 1983.

Nasr, Kamal S., *Business laws and taxation in Saudi Arabia*, Riyadh, 1979.

National Bank of Kuwait, *Economic and Financial Quarterly*.

Presley, John, 'The development of commercial banking in Saudi Arabia', article in *Arab banking and finance handbook*, Falcon, Bahrain, 1983

Al Sairafi, Abdul Muttalib, 'A new era in Kuwaiti stockmarket', article in *Arab banking and finance handbook*, Falcon, Bahrain, 1985.

Saudi Arabian Monetary Agency, *Annual report*, Riyadh.

Sayigh, Yusuf, *The Arab economy*, Oxford University Press, Oxford, 1982.

Schotta, Charles, 'Islamic banking in the US: regulatory issues', in *The impact and role of Islamic banking in international finance: issues and prospects*, a conference of the US Arab Chamber of Commerce, 28 June 1985, New York.

Sirageldin, Ismail Abu Hamid, *Saudis in transition: the challenges of a changing labor market*, Oxford University Press, New York, 1984.

Wohlers-Scharf, T., 'Arab and Islamic banking', article in *Arab banking and finance handbook*, Falcon, Bahrain, 1983.

Wilson, Rodney, *Banking and finance in the Arab Middle East*, Macmillan, London, 1983.

Wilson, Rodney, 'Arab banking in the Gulf: trends and prospects', article in *Arab banking and finance handbook*, Falcon, Bahrain, 1983.

MAGAZINES, NEWSPAPERS AND SPECIAL REPORTS

Arab Banking and Finance, London, published between 1983 and 1985.

Financial Times, London, special reports on Saudi, Kuwait and Bahrain.

Middle East Economic Survey, Nicosia, Cyprus.

Middle East Economic Digest, London, magazine and special surveys on Saudi Arabia, Kuwait and Bahrain since 1980.

Middle East Executive Reports, Washington, USA.

Middle East Money, London.

Index